KISSED BY THE KING

LESLIE GUSTAFSON

Scriptures referred to in this book are taken from the
most up to date translations of the Holy Bible
published by Zondervan Publishing House and
provided online by Biblegateway.com.

First Paperback Edition, January 2022

Manufactured in the United States of America

Cover by David Munoz

Published by Victory Vision Publishing and
Consulting
www.victoryvision.org

ISBN: 978-0-578-32933-8

DEDICATION

Thank you to my incredibly wonderful husband, John, for encouraging me and believing in me; our daughters, Raelyn and Abbie, for filling my life with joy; my mom for editing and being the best cheerleader a daughter could have; and all my family and friends for encouraging me to step out in faith and write this book.

I love each and every one of you!

CONTENTS

PREFACE

Kissed by the King stems from a personal journey of learning to walk in victory and rest in the unconditional love of our Heavenly Father. It comes from the realization that we are empowered, through God's Spirit, and can step out in faith and believe what He tells us in His Word. God's Word is alive. As we open its pages and learn to listen to His voice, He will transform our lives. I know because it is through His Word, resting in Christ's sacrifice, and learning to trust Him that He has transformed mine.

God has created each of us to be unique. Our lives will not and should not look exactly the same. Oh, the Spirit is the same, but the gifts and how He uses them may look different. He has a plan for each of our lives, and it is for good. One of the ways God has designed me is to see life situations in analogies. An everyday occurrence will happen, and God's Spirit will connect it to His Word in my heart. It took me a long time to realize that not everyone was hearing His voice in this way. However, it's okay, because I won't necessarily hear it the way He speaks to you. It doesn't mean we can't understand each other's language; it just means our relationship with our Dad is personal. As I learn to accept who He has made me to be, it frees me to accept who He has made you to be also.

It is through our personal relationship with Jesus that we have the joy of experiencing Him daily. Years ago, I was given some wonderful advice. I was told that part of living a life of victory and freedom in Jesus would come from living a lifestyle of worshipping Him. I didn't really have a clue what that meant. So, I began to dig into the Word and ask God to show me. I discovered that worshipping God is a daily opportunity. It is seeing Him in the gifts He sends our way. The moments each day when He taps us on the shoulder and whispers, "That was me. I love you!" The definition of worship includes the term kiss. While worship is something we offer to God (aka we give Him the kisses), I felt God stir something in my spirit that has changed how I look at everyday life. He likes to give me kisses as well. His kisses are not Him worshipping me, they are Him loving me. They are the little things and the big things. They are the moments your husband leaves a little note on the stove (explained in a devotion) that reminds you how very loved you are. They are the moments your child (or student) hands you a beautiful rock they picked up and you know it's a priceless treasure given in love. It's the sunsets, the family reunions, the learning of lessons, the presence of a friend during a difficult time, and the unexpected phone call which reminds us that we are loved. We are loved by the very God who spoke the world into existence. He sees us. He is alive, active, and speaking to us. He is the One sending us those gifts. Those are moments when we are being kissed by our King.

It is my prayer that as you read the devotions written within this book that you, too, will begin to identify moments when you are being kissed by the King. I pray you will hear His voice as He speaks to you. I pray that you embrace the relationship He yearns to have with you and receive the love He is sending you each day. Perfect love casts out fear, and the more we experience His love each day, the more freedom and victory we will walk in. And as you receive His love, as you tell Him thank you, as you return that love, and as you live life loved, He will be glorified through you. I pray today that you, too, are experiencing the joy of being kissed by the King.

SLOW DOWN

Do you ever wake up in the morning with your mind already racing? Let's see. I need to remember to add an additional piece of paperwork to the summer mailing, get my hair cut, go to the chiropractor, work on my homework, get groceries, stop at the bank, and for some reason, I'm already irritated that I'm not even out of bed yet. (I'm just being honest here.)

Do you ever have one of those days? I remained in bed awhile and started up a conversation with the Lord. I was completely honest and told Him I was rather tired of having my mind spin like this. And guess what came to me? I sat there and thought to myself, "I haven't been in the Word since I got home." Then I thought, "Last time I went too long without being in the Word, I got all anxious and irritable also."

So, I got up and mixed my power drink, grabbed a breakfast bar, sat in the recliner, and jumped into the Word. It was just what I needed. Well, truth be told, HE was just WHO I needed. Getting into the Word allowed a soothing salve to be wiped over my thoughts and emotions. It helped me to set my mind on things above and not on earthly things. Remembering how much Jesus loves me and how special I am to Him set my heart at peace. You see, it's spending time WITH Him that brings both of us joy. He's my best friend. He's got my life completely under control. He enjoys hanging out with me.

Just like we help our best friends out when they need it, He's willing to help us out too. Way too often, I try to manhandle life and then give Him a shout-out when I've made a bit of a mess of things. Or I say yes to one too many things because I want to keep everyone happy. Or even worse, I don't want to be judged for what I'm not doing. Inevitably, the feeling of being overwhelmed and anxious comes knocking on the door of my heart. You see, when I sit with my Best Friend, I already know I'm loved. I already know that I'm accepted. I can tell people no because I don't have to fear being abandoned or alone. And it's not just telling people no. It's telling people yes. It's really about trusting Jesus and being obedient. After hanging out with Him for a while, He will offer clarity and direction. He will provide a sense of peace when I'm going the right way. He will help calm my thoughts and just take the next step needed for that day. Each thing I did today ended up being a joy. Because we did them together. Calmly.

"And whatever you do, in word or deed, do everything in the name of the Lord Jesus, giving thanks to God the Father through him." Colossians 3:17

"Martha, Martha," the Lord answered, "you are worried and upset about many things, but few things are needed—or indeed only one. Mary has chosen what is better, and it will not be taken away from her." Luke 10:41-42

SMACK GOES THE
APPLE TREE

The Lord is really using the apple tree this summer. Unfortunately, yesterday's lesson seemed a bit "harder" to learn. I was out mowing and was quite happy in my own little world. It's so strange that when I wear my sunglasses it feels like the rest of the world doesn't really exist. And, WHAM, I hit a very unforgiving branch on the apple tree. It didn't give. Well, if it did, I didn't feel it give. It hurt. And, yes, I did what I did. I got angry and cried.

Suddenly, I was telling the Lord absolutely everything that was wrong in my life. I was mowing alone. I mean, really? Where was everyone else anyway? My head hurt, I was alone, the bugs had instantaneously started to bite me, the wind was in the wrong direction and all the grass was blowing back in my face, and for heaven's sake, why didn't "someone" prune the apple tree?

And, just like the smack on the head, I was hit hard by how quickly I spiraled. Really? Was I complaining to the Lord, because someone didn't prune the apple tree? (Side note: The apple tree WAS pruned, and because there was so much fruit, the branch was hanging lower than usual... another lesson.) Self-pity had come to visit just because I'd bumped my head when I forgot to duck. Wow! Scripture says out of the heart, the mouth speaks, and clearly, I had some heart issues going on that needed to be addressed. But here's the great thing. The darkness hates the Light because the Light exposes the darkness. (John 3:20) As soon as I brought all that anger to the Lord, He turned it to praise. Like, thank you, Lord, I wasn't using a push mower; we have a beautiful big green lawn that needs mowing; the family is healthy and otherwise engaged; I love mowing and don't mind being out there alone; the birds were singing, and I live in the country so I get to hear them when the mower isn't running; and at least the knock in the head didn't catapult me off the lawn mower. God is in the business of changing hearts. And, when the Light entered into the anger and self-pity, He turned it around. The darkness lost its power when the Light exposed it. He proved that on the cross. He wants us to bring Him our hurts and anger. He loves to bring healing and restoration. And, sometimes, a good smack in the head shakes loose the lies we're believing so He can address them with grace. God is so very good! And friends, please duck!

LAWN MOWER

Last year, as we neared the end of the mowing season, it became apparent that we may need to upgrade our lawn mower. So, as spring approached this year, John began doing his research. I wasn't surprised to come home one day and have him tell me a new mower would be arriving at the end of the week. Yay! This would be a tremendous blessing considering the size of the lawn and the assistance with Abbie mowing the cemetery.

You know the feeling when you get something new and can't wait to use it? You know, because your life is going to be better, easier, and things will run more smoothly. Umm, not always. You see, our wonderful new lawn mower was a zero turn. Have you ever tried one? Well, I had. Several years ago, we test drove a zero turn and after running into a tree while attempting to maneuver it, I thought I had made myself **very** clear that I had no intention of ever driving one again. No thank you, sir. I'll take a steering wheel if you please.

We've now had our lawnmower for about three months. I spent the first two driving the old lawn mower around. John would hop on the new one (it did look nice because he could get closer to the trees), and I'd putz on the smaller one. One day I decided I was being silly, so I headed out to the shed to give it a whirl. I didn't tell anyone, but apparently, John heard me attempting to start it. (Who knew? Push this lever, pull the throttle, push that down, pull the handles in and ignore the thing that looks like a brake, because apparently, it is simply decor.) I did get it started. And it died. I got it started again, and by this time my husband had arrived on the scene. Yep, just in time to watch me heading, headlong towards the wall of his machine shed. He's yelling "stop," and I'm yelling, "I can't!" Once I managed to get the thing stopped, I hopped off and stomped out of the shed like any mature 51-year-old woman would. (No machine sheds were harmed in the making of this devotion.)

Well, that put a quick end to my decision and John's willingness to allow me to use the new lawn mower. Until about three weeks ago. Abbie had the old mower at the cemetery, and I needed to get after our yard. I had one option. John happened to still be home so I asked (very sweetly) if he would **teach** me **how** to run the lawn mower. He agreed (hesitantly) and only under the condition he got to drive it out of the machine shed for me. And I then had to practice in the wide open space and drive very, very slowly. Sigh.

You know, those things tend to have a mind of their own. I started out trying to figure out which hand needs to go which way to turn, back up, etc. And today, after mowing with it for a handful of weeks, it's as if I've always known how. Guess how you do it? You don't think! You drive by instinct. If I stop and try to think about what to do with my arms, I end up going in circles at top speed. If I just let my body do what it knows it needs to, all goes fine.

As I was riding on the mower today, it struck me how very much like our spiritual life this new mower has been. How? We need to stop overthinking everything! There is a reason Scripture tells us in 2 Corinthians 10:5 to demolish arguments and every pretension that sets itself up against the knowledge of God and take captive every thought to make it obedient to Christ. Because when we start listening to the lies floating around and ignore the Truth of the Gospel, we're almost guaranteed a crash of some sort.

You know the kind I'm talking about, right? Remember the lady who looked at you funny at the grocery store? You went home certain she must be annoyed with you, or you decided maybe she was just a nasty person. When, in all reality, she was thinking about her doctor's appointment and didn't even see you. Or what about your boss who was short tempered with you? You allowed a tone you were spoken in to convince you that you are unloved and unworthy. Yet maybe they just had an argument with their spouse and took it out on you. What about a mistake you really did make? You're a failure? Nope, you're imperfect and forgiven. Or the ultimate ones, the ones we tell ourselves. I'm not pretty enough. I'm not funny enough. Etc. Etc. As long as we let that negative garbage run around in our heads, we're setting ourselves up to be controlled by something other than the Truth.

How do we recognize it? How do you know Truth from lies? Well, just as I needed to run the lawn mower by instinct, we need to listen to the Holy Spirit. He will prompt us. As you fill yourself with the Word, He will bring it to your mind when needed. His fruit is love, joy, peace, patience, kindness, gentleness, goodness, faithfulness, and self-control. If what you're thinking about doesn't bear this fruit, you're quite likely dwelling on a lie. And lies have a way of stirring you into behaviors you don't really want to be demonstrating. The Truth is always, always found in Scripture. If it isn't in there, don't believe it about yourself. If the enemy tries to tell you you're a failure, remember you are a child of God. Not feeling loved? Well, Jesus loved you enough to die for you. Rejected? Oh, He's covered that, too. You're accepted and redeemed.

As you head about the rest of your day, remember, don't overthink the little things. "Finally, brothers and sisters, whatever is true, whatever is noble, whatever is right, whatever is pure, whatever is lovely, whatever is admirable--if anything is excellent or praiseworthy--think about such things." Philippians 4:8

GOD'S GLORY

Do you ever wake up to a song playing over and over in your mind? Today the song by Jesus Culture playing for me had the verse, "Show us, show us Your glory. Show us, show us Your glory. Show us, show us Your glory, Lord!" I sat at my kitchen counter saying, "Okay, Lord, are You going to show me Your glory?" And the response was, "Are you going to pay attention when I do?" (Full disclosure, I was praying for something specific, and He was gently and lovingly reminding me that His glory was foremost. Oh, those humbling moments.)

How often do we charge into our day and don't give a second thought to where God plans to reveal Himself? He is all over. His glory is everywhere. The question remains, "Do I stop and pay attention long enough to see it?" Yesterday, one of my students came walking in, and the first thing they wanted to tell me was about the nightmare they had. It was clearly very troubling to the child, because this was several hours later, and they were still trying to process it. We had a talk about what we can do when we wake up from a nightmare. I encouraged them to begin praying right away. I wish I had shared that just saying the name Jesus over and over has power. I know there are times when I am afraid, and it is all I can do to squeak out one word. And if we only get one word, I believe that's the best one to choose. ("... that at the name of Jesus every

knee should bow, in heaven and on earth and under the earth..."
Philippians 2:10)

As we were having this discussion, a fellow classmate revealed that they actually sleep with their Bible every night. Wow! A four-year-old knows "...in the beginning was the Word and the Word was with God and the Word was God." He trusts the power of God's Word and knows that sleeping with God's Word close will bring peace and total rest. Do you believe it, too? Do you trust it? Do you allow your last thought before you hit the pillow to be one of God's promises? Did you awake this morning looking for His glory? I know it was there. And once you see it, it will fill your day! Your heart will overflow with love and spread into the lives of others. It's an inner beauty which radiates to those around and warms their very being.

As far as seeing God's glory today, I want to make a side note that it was everywhere. The pond was gorgeous this morning as I drove out the lane. The fog was hovering over it a bit and the briskness made it sparkle. (Shocking that His glory is in winter too!) The sunrise was stunning. And after the last children left the building today, and I was walking back to the classroom, the door opened, and two students came sprinting back inside. I asked if they had forgotten something and was met with, "We forgot to give you goodbye hugs!" What a great way to end my work week! God's glory was revealed through the demonstration of love by His children. Oh, Jesus, may I glorify You by sharing Your love with others the same way!

As you head to bed tonight and when you rise in the morning, I challenge you to fill yourself with the promises of God. As you walk in faith trusting and obeying His Word, He will be glorified through your life. I can't imagine a better legacy to leave than a life that glorifies the Lord!

GOD'S PLANS

"*Now* it happened after the death of Moses the servant of the Lord, that the Lord spoke to Joshua the son of Nun, Moses' servant, saying 'Moses My servant is dead; now therefore arise, cross over this Jordan, you and all this people, into the land which I am giving to them, to the sons of Israel.
I have given you every place on which the sole of your foot treads, just as I promised to Moses.'"
Joshua 1:1-3

Isn't this a powerful Scripture? Moses had a huge job. He was called to lead God's people out of captivity. Can you even imagine attempting to lead that large of a group of people without cell phones, mass texting, and social media? I know the challenge of keeping a group of four-year-olds in a straight line. The idea of thousands and thousands of people following wherever you are going is mind boggling. A tremendous responsibility. Yet God empowered Him to do it!

You would think after doing all that work, it would be Moses who would lead the Israelites into the Promised Land. But as I read the Scripture above, I was struck by the difference in responsibility God had for Moses and Joshua. (I am aware there is more to the story.) God used Moses to lead the people out of slavery. Joshua's job was to escort them into the land God had given them. Both leaders. Both called by God. Both willing to do what God had called them to do. And check out the promise. Wow! I mean, really, wow! "I have given you every place on which the sole of your foot treads. (Joshua 1:3)" How is that for a promise as Joshua headed into battle? God is going to give him every place his foot treads. It doesn't mean he won't face battles, but he does know in advance who will be victorious in the battle.

We are living in a time where the battle is becoming more intense daily. The Word of God is clear that "... we are not fighting against flesh-and-blood enemies, but against evil rulers and authorities of the unseen world, against mighty powers in this dark world, and against evil spirits in the heavenly places (Ephesians 6:12)." As believers we are being called into God's battle. While it is important to know where our battle is being played out, it is imperative that we rest assured understanding that God has given us authority every place our feet tread in His fight. We already know who is going to win. Or should I say, **Who** has already won?

In Luke 10:19 God tells us clearly, "I have given you authority to trample on snakes and scorpions and to overcome all the power of the enemy; nothing will harm you. (NIV)" God's got a plan for you. He has called you. Whatever sphere of life He has you in, it is not by accident. He will empower you to fulfill whatever calling He has placed on you. It will be for His glory and the furthering of His kingdom. And the reality of the situation is that if we want to live in the Promised Land God has for us, it will likely require us to engage in a spiritual battle. We no longer have to live a life of mediocrity, one devoid of hope or joy. We belong to the Ruler and Creator of the universe! We get to live in victory.

"... Let us throw off everything that hinders and the sin that so easily entangles..." (Hebrews 12:1) and pick up our swords

(Ephesians 6:17). We've got to get into our Word and get on our knees. This battle is going to be fought in prayer (vs 19), being bold in sharing the Gospel (vs 19) and standing (vs 13).

"... for the battle is the Lord's, and he will give all of you into our hands." (1 Samuel 17:47b)

OFF THEY GO

Every year for the past twenty years, we've sent someone in the house off to their first day of school (excluding my choice of livelihood). When the girls were young, it always meant a fun trip to WalMart™ or Target™ to stock up on new and glittery school supplies. Often there was a new backpack hanging on the chair and perhaps a new pair of shoes to escort the little feet into school. As they have grown older, the girls' needs changed, and the folders turned into fancy calculators and more practical three-ring binders. Planners were purchased to track where to be next and what time. And cars were added to the driveway to get everyone where they needed to be safely.

Today marks something new. Today is the last time we will send a child off to school. Our baby heads back to college to finish her senior year. It's the last time we watch someone load up their vehicle and drive out the lane to further their education. (Although John suspects someone will land back here eventually during a transition and the door is always open.) Even though both girls are adults, there is always a spot in the heart that tugs a bit. Whether they are heading back to college or driving back to their apartment, it's bittersweet to watch them walk out the door. The old saying is true; it's like having your heart walk around outside your body.

However, today I am grateful. Because as I reflect upon the joy each of our daughters has brought into our lives, I am reminded that God's love is even greater than ours. As He watches us and walks with us, His heart swells with love. I wonder if His heart aches just a little at the intensity of it all. We started out babes in His arms. We first began our walk with Him, and our faith was fresh and overwhelming. As we grow in our knowledge and love for Jesus, the relationship deepens. Just as we journey with our children through their ups and downs of life. Just as our heart aches when they have pain. So must the Father's. His love is so intense He gave His Son for us. And yet, His love does not change. Over the years, whether our children were graciously doing what we asked the first time or dumping cereal all over the living room floor, they were still loved. Oh, just like we had to discipline the cereal incident, God loves us enough to discipline us. He wants us to flourish, to shine brighter for Him, to know His love and trust His heart for us.

Today as you go about your business, remember that wonderful Truth. God loves you. There is nothing you can do that will change that reality. You are His child. He feels the same joy, the same pain, and craves time with you just as you do your own children. If you're questioning whether it's true, go check out John 3:16. "For God so loved the world that he gave his one and only Son, that whoever believes in him shall not perish but have eternal life." He loved us enough to give His Son for us. It's a love well worth trusting.

15

MICE CLIMBING TREES

It's true. We never stop learning. Today I was outside and saw something I'd never seen before and had no idea that could happen. I watched a mouse run up a tree. Did you know mice could climb trees? If you're a mouse lover, you may want to stop reading. I'm not a mouse lover, and I'm here to say, I was a little grossed out. I have no idea why, but I just didn't think mice could or should climb trees. I guess I don't know what I thought they did all day, but climbing trees was not on the list I would have written out. (You know, the list someone was sure to have me write about mice.)

Well, I've been thinking about that mouse. And for some reason, I haven't been able to shake the astonishment that he had that little skill I knew nothing about. We didn't have mice in the house growing up so I haven't ever really heard them in the walls, but I know other people have discussed it, and it should have clicked that they can climb. But a tree? Really? A tree? (And, just an FYI, he went way up there until I quit watching.) I think the little guy ran up there because it was trying to get away from me. Wise decision. At first, I thought this devotion would take the direction of people having gifts and talents that we know nothing about. I was going to challenge you not to put yourself in a box. You or someone you know may have a hidden gift. Seek the Lord. Ask Him what He wants you to do with it. (Mini lesson) But, surprisingly, those aren't the questions I'm going to ask.

No, what strikes me even more is that the mouse was likely running for cover. It's quite probable that I was demolishing his nest with the lawn mower. And what is now rolling around in my spirit is the question, "What are you running from?" Have you felt under attack lately? Is it coming at you from all sides? Or is it maybe just one side? One person. One situation. Someone you just can't seem to connect with even though you've tried. You see them coming and head for your tree. Oh, trust me, I don't think you're **really** climbing a tree. But what does your "tree" look like? Do you withdraw into yourself? Does your wall go up so you're present in body but not engaged? Have you convinced yourself there is something wrong with you? Or them? (Most likely them, right?)

When our daughters were in high school, they took a psychology test in which one of the questions was, "If you saw a bear, what would you do?" My initial response was to run. Although further reflection tells me that would be unwise, because I'd quite likely end up lunch meat. My little brother's response was, "I'd stand and watch it." Then he proceeded to tell me there were all sorts of dynamics, and he needed more information. The funny thing about it was that question was supposed to indicate how you handle conflict. I do have a tendency to avoid conflict. (There was a reason I was good at track.) Where my brother handles conflict exactly like he responded. He'll watch it. Or remove himself from it if it doesn't pertain to him. Or confront it head on. He's not reactive. Anyway, what would you do? How do you handle conflict? What do you do when you sense emotional danger? Do you climb the tree like the mouse? Do you run? Remove yourself? The bigger question, are you handling it in a godly way which glorifies Christ?

Obedience is following God's way. Sometimes He will ask us to forgive and move on. Sometimes, if you're in immediate danger, He may remove you from the situation until you're safe and can gain perspective. Most likely He will ask you to pursue Matthew 18:15 "If another believer sins against you, go privately and point out the offense. If the other person listens and confesses it, you have won that person back. "As much as you may hate conflict, it is quite likely driven by fear if you're avoiding it. You'll have to seek the Lord for the root of the fear. However, God did not give us a spirit of fear. Rather, 1 Timothy 1:7 reminds us, "He gave us a spirit of power, love, and a sound mind." Don't back down. Don't run for the cover of the tree. Stand firm. Seek to maintain the relationship. The devil loves to destroy relationships, especially those between believers. After all, if he can get the church fighting among itself, it's not going to appear a very attractive place for someone who doesn't know Jesus. John 13:35 says, "By this everyone will know that you are my disciples, if you love one another." Sometimes love requires us to walk through a conflict. All the time it requires forgiveness. And, if you happen to be hanging out in a tree avoiding something right now, I'd encourage you to come down. God will walk you through whatever you're currently fearing. Because "... greater is God who is in you than he who is in the world." (1 John 4:4)

THE SQUIRREL

T he other day on the way to work, a squirrel went running across the highway. It had an ear of corn in its mouth. It didn't look at the cars driving by, and it didn't slow down. He had his eyes set on the trees at the park, and there was no stopping him until he reached his destination. I happened to be turning the corner and slowed down to watch and see where it went. It headed up a tree with the corn still in its mouth.

I don't know if I've ever seen a squirrel with an entire ear of corn, and I was especially surprised with the time of year he was running with it. For some reason, I would have envisioned the corn being collected in the Fall after the harvest. Instead, here we are in the Spring, and he was able to find the corn in the field across the road, pick it up, and carry it back to his home to eat at his convenience.

The image of that squirrel has really stuck with me. The first thought that ran through my mind was the importance of getting our "food." The squirrel didn't go to a restaurant and order his meal; he went searching for it and brought it home. I'm going to guess he was hungry, or else he wouldn't have risked running across the road in the first place. The second image was his determination. The little guy never wavered when he saw the traffic. He had his corn, his destination, and nothing was going to deter his mission. It was to get the food where it needed to be at the risk of his own life.

Can you see where this is going before I even make the connection? The squirrel was hungry. I don't think he would have gone looking for food otherwise. He knew he NEEDED the food to survive. And he didn't just eat it in the field but instead took it home where he could continue to eat it and be fed. What about you? Are you spiritually hungry? Do you have a desire to know Jesus? Are you wanting to be fed? Are you willing to seek out what He has for you? Are you willing to take it home and feast on it every day? Or, how about multiple times a day?

Years ago a friend and I were discussing church, and she shared a very insightful truth. She said, "Would you only eat once a week? Why then would we think one day a week at church is enough to keep us fed?" Well, I confess that was a sobering thought. It may have even stung a bit. But the truth of it has stayed with me all these years. There is no way hearing the Word once a week would be enough to keep me fed. How about you? Do you find yourself getting hungry during the week? Do you end up filling up on "spiritual junk food" instead of the meat and potatoes of God's Word (aka anything we turn to in order to meet our needs that don't include Jesus)? Are you willing to take responsibility for your spiritual health and growth? Church is amazing. I wouldn't trade the fellowship and time of worship. However, it's not enough to keep my soul fed and nourished all week long.

The other thing which amazed me in watching that squirrel was his determination to get across that road. His eyes were set on getting the food to its destination. I assumed it was for himself, and he was taking it home. But he could have been sharing it, I suppose. Are we willing to go after our spiritual food and bring it into our homes with unwavering determination? Will you seek it out for yourself? Your children? Your spouse? Will you share it with your neighbor and friends? What about your co-worker who isn't a believer? Are you willing to carry the Word where it needs to be and not get distracted by the cars going by? Is your determination to deliver Jesus to others all-consuming?

The thing is, eternity is forever, but life is not. We can get to going about our lives and think today's concerns are the most pressing. However, sometimes we just need a perspective check. Is what you are worrying about today really an eternal issue? Do you know someone who is viewing a life circumstance from an earthly perspective versus a heavenly one? What would happen if you dug into the Word to see what God has to say about it? Would it change your view? Your choices? Go grab some corn. Eat it. Share it. Sit with Jesus and hang out awhile. He will change your life, I promise!

John 6:33-35
"For the bread of God is that which comes down out of heaven, and gives life to the world." Then they said to Him, "Lord, always give us this bread." Jesus said to them, "I am the bread of life; he who comes to Me will not hunger, and he who believes in Me will never thirst.

Deuteronomy 8:3
"He humbled you and let you be hungry, and fed you with manna which you did not know, nor did your fathers know, that He might make you understand that man does not live by bread alone, but man lives by everything that proceeds out of the mouth of the LORD.

Matthew 5:6
"Blessed are those who hunger and thirst for righteousness, for they shall be satisfied.

Psalm 42:2

My soul thirsts for God, for the living God; When shall I come
and appear before God?

HAMSTER WHEEL

"The sting of death is sin, and the power of sin is the law; but thanks be to God, who gives us the victory through our Lord Jesus Christ." 1 Corinthians 15:56-57

During my first year of teaching, I went up to my classroom after a ball game and could hear a strange noise down the hallway. Okay, yes, I was scared. It was dark, and the building was old. You can imagine what I built it up to be in my mind. (Because, of course, burglars and scary people make big loud noises during the night in school buildings.) As I entered my classroom, I discovered the noise to be our class hamster. He was on his wheel and going around and around. The squeak of the wheel was making enough noise down the hall to create quite a racket and terrify one's imagination in the dark. Well, I did what any unsettled first year teacher would do, I unhooked the wheel from the side of the cage. And when I left, I didn't put it back up. Not only did it feel much more relaxing shutting the lights off without the noise, the error in judgement with the wheel allowed the hamster to escape. Needless to say, there could still be a hamster running around that school and by now he's likely a GIANT hamster!

The reason this story came to mind is because as I reflected upon my previous week, I realized I felt like the hamster must have felt on his wheel. My mind was going a hundred miles an hour. I had allowed it to become flooded with the emotions of homework, feelings of inadequacy, and fear. How quickly I found myself going round and round. I knew it was spilling over into my health as I felt myself begin to become stuck in flight-or-fright mode. But knowing something is happening and stopping it are two very different things.

It wasn't until yesterday morning that I took the time to sit down with my Bible and take it before the Lord. (Did I mention sometimes when I get that way, I tend to begin ditching my morning time with Jesus? Sigh.) He is the One Person I need the most, and He can be Who I set aside. And He did what He always does. He met me at the kitchen counter. (It's not always at the counter, but on school days it's usually our place.) Loud and clear. Fear. I hadn't even recognized it come a-knocking. But all those things I was stressing over were fear based. And we all know fear isn't from God. At least not this kind of fear. This fear was being given power because it was rooted in the Law. The law. Ugh! Why does it seem like a place that wants to draw us back in?

The Good News in this story is Jesus took the hamster wheel down and gave us victory. He died. Literally, He died. He Who created the world, Who was there at creation allowed Himself to be hung on a cross in my place. In your place, too. All our fears, guilt, and shame were pounded into those nails and defeated as Christ rose from the dead. We now have freedom, joy, and peace. We can set our anxieties at the foot of the cross (or the rock by the tomb) and embrace the gift of eternity.

Sorry, I know today's devotion is a little long. I tried to forewarn you that I was going to be processing out loud. And, as I do, I'm near tears. Because I want you to know that Jesus is everything. He meets us in the darkness and sets us free. Whatever sin you're fighting today, He can handle. And that sin can be triggered by an emotion. The pain you may be feeling isn't the sin. It's what you do with it. Take what you're carrying and hand it to Jesus. Envision yourself as His child walking along holding His hand. You can't hold the sin and His hand at the same time. (And, no, you may not shift it to the other hand. It's too heavy to carry one-handed.) Embrace the freedom He is offering. He will walk you through whatever you are dealing with. "You will know the Truth and the Truth will set you free. (John 8:32)" You are not defined by your current circumstances. And you certainly do not need to live in fear. You can rest knowing the One Who defeated law at the cross. "O Death, where is your victory? O death, where is your sting? (1 Corinthians 15:55)"

Hop off that hamster wheel today. Fix your eyes upon Jesus and remember sin has no power under grace.

STOP COMPARING

This morning as we headed out the garage door for church, we commented on the tomato plants in the pot right outside the door. We have two pots, and both have two plants. The plants in the closest pot are much taller and fuller. It is covered with flowers and has almost reached the top of our deck. However, John made the observation that for as tall as it is he wasn't seeing many tomatoes on it yet. The other plant is shorter, much less full in appearance, but we could see tomatoes.

As we drove to church, we wondered about the growth of the one pot versus the other. Someone (sorry, we can't remember who) told us the more you water a tomato plant the bigger it gets. Because this pot is closer to the spigot, we wondered if it was getting more water. Yet, it didn't appear that the height or fullness of the tomato determined the amount of fruit it bore. Of course, knowing the way my mind works, it led me to consider whether it is a reflection of our spiritual lives. Are there times when our lives appear to be full and growing when in reality there is less fruit? Is it in the times when things seem a bit sparse and thin that our fruit can be seen? We cling to Jesus, hold tight, and He bears fruit.

Later, I noticed that the big plant was also actually covered with fruit. The more we water a plant, perhaps it does bear more fruit. Am I watering my soul? Am I in the Word? Do I want a relationship with Jesus that is full, green, lush, bearing much fruit? I want to grow and spill over with the joy of Jesus. I want to be armed and ready during the seasons where life feels a bit dry, yet His love grows fruit. More importantly, I just want to be with Him every single day. Walking filled with His love and, therefore, bearing the fruit of that love.

FUEL UP

Today, I went to put fuel in a car I'm not used to driving. I pulled in and had to keep telling myself, "The tank is on the other side, Leslie." I got out and proceeded to put the nozzle in and noticed the gas cap says E85. (The thought ran through my head that maybe I should call John and see what that means before I filled the vehicle.) However, I rarely tend to follow through on those types of thoughts until well after the fact. (God is still working out the fruit of patience in my life!)

After finishing filling the tank, I got in the car and then called John. (See, I did follow through, maybe just not in the correct order at times.) I explained the gas cap scenario. (Have I ever mentioned I am married to a **VERY** patient and calm man? God knew just who I needed to balance me.) Whew, all was good. I had the option to put in E85, but I could also use what I did. Off I went to meet my relatives for lunch. As I was chatting with my cousin about it later, she said she has to keep reminding herself that she needs diesel fuel when she fills up. Apparently, they had also traded vehicles, and it was taking time to adjust to the change. We both wholeheartedly agreed that our primary concern was not to use the wrong fuel, because we didn't want to ruin the motors in our vehicles.

Hmm, what gas does your motor require? Oh, I don't want to know what type of gasoline your car or truck takes. I want to know what type of "fuel" your spirit requires. If you want your life to run correctly, you have to energize yourself with the proper propellant. God wants to be your source. He wants to fill us with His Spirit and direct our paths. This will only come from being in His Word on a regular and consistent basis. If you attempt to fill your spirit with anything other than Him, odds are good you may blow up your engine.

Ephesians 5:18 says, "And do not get drunk with wine, for that is dissipation, but be filled with the Spirit," Matthew 4:4, "Jesus answered, "It is written: 'Man shall not live on bread alone, but on every word that comes from the mouth of God." These are just two examples of things people try to fill their life with other than God and His Spirit. Do you run to food? (If I'm honest, chocolate and carbohydrates are a go-to in times of stress.) What about the alcohol He was referring to in Ephesians? Is it shopping? Gossip? Fear and worry? Perhaps you are always looking for a new friend or relationship to fill that empty tank? Or maybe yours is work? Busyness? You know yourself the best. I hope in your honest reflection, you can stand and say, "Nope, I'm filling myself with God, His Word, His Spirit, and the love of my Savior." However, if the answer in your blank is something else, maybe now would be a good time to have a chat with the Father. Ask His Spirit to lead you and guide you. Ask Him to reveal to you anything that is preventing your tank from being filled with Him. And if you're new at surrendering the old to make room for the new, don't wallow in condemnation. God says in Romans 8 that "there is now no condemnation for those who are in Christ Jesus." Just keep reminding yourself (better yet, trust the Holy Spirit to remind you) that you run on a new type of fuel. Your energy and power come from the Spirit of the Living God, the same Who rose Jesus our Savior from the grave and seated Him at the right hand of our God and Father. This is the same Spirit who now lives on inside you. Did you hear that? He is residing on the inside of you! He is waiting to fill your tank with the right fuel. All you need to do is ask. Surrender the old. Remind yourself you need a new kind of fuel. And power up!

THE SON GROWS
THE GRASS

The last two days in Iowa have been rainy, dark, and gloomy. It's been hard to be excited about much of anything with the weather weighing us down. Last night we were even treated to a good ol' spring thunderstorm. I usually love them, but I was pretty much done with blah weather by then. But, hey, we live in a state where things don't ever stay the same. We were treated this morning to bright sunshine streaming through the window and green grass all over the yard!

What a perfect representation of the current season of America. Our lives have changed in the past couple of weeks with quarantines and social distancing. It can feel like we are in a storm. Yet we have the hope of Sonshine! We know when we wake up the Son will still remain consistent in our hearts. His love and care are a constant. He refreshes us anew and just like that we have new life in Him.

As I sit here on the sofa and look out the window, our lawn is covered with last year's leaves and the branches from freshly pruned trees. I can see the green grass everywhere except underneath the leaves and sticks. What's under those leaves? Life! We have been set free in Jesus, but just like the grass, it will take time for our outsides to match up with what's inside. You may have growth in some areas with life flowing, but others may still be covered and not seen as clearly. But there IS still life underneath. It's just not been exposed yet. God will expose it, and it will be for His glory!

It's good to remember condemnation is not from God. He's not telling you to shape up and get it together. No, He's going to send help to remove the debris from your spiritual life. Just as we are saved by grace, we are changed by grace. Perhaps you will receive new life and deliverance immediately. Or, perhaps you will get to experience the bristle of the rake as it slides over sin, and God begins to pile it up and burns it in His refinement of you. I know beyond a shadow of a doubt, as we walk more fully conscious and aware of His vast love for us, our behaviors and actions will follow. "Because, where our treasure is, there will our heart be also. (Matthew 6:21)" What sin are you holding onto because it's filling a need to be loved? Needed? Wanted? Safer? Let His love replace it even if the process is slow in coming.

Are you allowing today's storm to turn you green? Are you willing to let it turn you to Jesus in a new way? Are you seeking Him? Do you feel like He isn't listening? Are you willing to trust even when life doesn't seem to "make sense?" We can't see the future the way He does. We can't know what He is protecting us from. Or teaching us. We don't have a clue what better He may have for us. We do know that "God works all things for the good of those who love him and are called according to His purpose. (Romans 8:28)" Just wait! The sun will come out, and your grass will grow. Give it time. He's not giving up on you, so don't give up on Him! He loves you! He proved it at the cross!

KNOW YOUR
MISSION

Have you ever watched a toddler walk? Don't you love how they waddle? It isn't the steady gait of a young child yet, but they know where they want to go and almost mimic a penguin in their approach to the world. I was watching a little girl the other day who was busily moving back and forth and around and around. She stopped right in front of me and proceeded to remove the "closed" sign that was attached to a string beside where I was standing. She handed it to me with a determined look. I smiled, thanked her, and asked if she could find any more. Off she went. She waddled to another sign, removed it, delivered it to our growing pile, and set off again to see if she could find another. What I loved about watching her was the longer she went the more determined she became. Her gentle removal of the paper signs turned into a big yank. She was gaining momentum, and her determination was growing. Rather than just removing the sign, she proceeded to pull down the string which was holding it as well. It was fascinating to watch. And encouraging. Why?

Revelation 3:16 says "So, because you are lukewarm--neither hot nor cold--I am about to spit you out of my mouth." I don't know about you, but the last place I want to be is flying through the air like a cannonball because I am lukewarm. Can you imagine being spit out of God's mouth? Umm, no thank you! I'd rather curl up on His lap and be reassured and loved like His child. Do you live your faith? Or have you become lukewarm in your approach to your walk with the Father? God wants to have a relationship with us. Daily. Moment by moment. He wants to be a part of the ups and the downs. Is He obvious? Evident? Can you see His fruit? Are others able to identify it? Do they know Who drives your decisions? Do you?

Why do I compare being lukewarm to the toddler? The more she waddled and removed signs (no worries, these were not road signs and laws were not being broken), the more her confidence in the mission grew. Do you feel like you've lost your mission? Have you lost your first love? Do you feel the fire of the Spirit has dimmed or grown cold? Has it been a while since you've taken time to sit with the Father and have your morning coffee? God is loving and kind. He is patient and is waiting for you to return. The more you sit and spend time with Him, the more confidence you will gain. Your heart will be at peace. Your life will produce fruit. Your mission will become clear. And praise Jesus, your confidence will grow! Your joy will return, and your fire will be contagious!

Perhaps none of this applies to you, and you won't connect with this devotion. I hope that is the case. The reality has been that it can be difficult to focus with all the angst in the world. Or maybe the angst has drawn you closer to Jesus than ever before. I hope that is the case. Or maybe you've not even noticed the anxiety of many around you. I encourage you today to enjoy time with the Father. Don't miss it. Make it a priority. Curl up on His lap and listen to what He has to say. Pray. Listen. Pray. Listen. Pray. Listen. And share the joy of Jesus with others! And then pray and listen some more! God is amazing. "The LORD is my light and my salvation--

whom shall I fear? The LORD is the stronghold of my life-- of whom shall I be afraid? (Psalm 27:1)"

ABORTED FRUIT

Have you ever had a couple of those super busy days? The kind where you open your eyes, and your feet barely have time to hit the floor before your body flies into action? I've had a couple of those lately. Friday felt like a whirlwind. I don't teach on Fridays, so my brain thinks it needs to get everything else finished that has been ignored all week. And yesterday was spent outside. We dug potatoes, mowed the yard (the parts that aren't dead), burned two huge piles of debris, and miscellaneous other things we found in the interim. At one point, I looked at my husband a bit irritably (you know the whole hands on your hips and snippy tone thing) to point out that he was in a crabby state of mind only to be met with his quick interpretation that **I** was the one in a mood. Stop. Think. Yep. Quite possible.

Now set aside that story for just a moment. Back up with me to about mid-July. John and I had been out in the yard and were finding fruit from our trees on the ground. Apples and peaches. I asked him about it, because it was way too early for the fruit to be ready and falling to the ground. He told me that without rain the trees were beginning to abort their fruit. The nutrients needed were just not available. It was really rather sobering to consider, and we began watering our trees so we didn't lose any more fruit.

Can you see how these two stories collided today? We were driving home from church, and he was telling me a chore we needed to get done. I said, "Are we going to get paid to do that, or are we just going to do it to be nice?"

His response, "We're just going to be nice." And then added sarcastically, "Yes, you can be nice." I quickly corrected him by pointing out that I am nice. I consider "nice" to be "a state of being." I'm always "nice." Because kindness is a fruit of the Holy Spirit Who lives in me. But, sometimes like Friday and Saturday, my "nice" gets aborted.

Just like our fruit trees need water to hold their fruit, we also need the nourishment of the Word of God and time spent with Him to hold our spiritual fruit. The Holy Spirit lives in us. He produces fruit. "... the fruit of the Spirit is love, joy, peace, forbearance, kindness, goodness, faithfulness, gentleness and self-control. Against such things there is no law. (Galatians 5:22-23)" If we aren't being watered with Him, we will begin to abort our fruit. We can become irritable. Our fruit lands on the ground and rots away. It doesn't get used. There is no opportunity for consumption. It can't be used to build up and nourish someone else.

Jesus was forever pouring Himself out to others. But He also took time to refill. "After he had dismissed them, he went up on a mountainside by himself to pray. (Matthew 14:23 [NIV])" He knew that spending time with the Father was imperative. He had to be replenished in His Spirit. Jesus was all God, but He was also all man so one can see where He, too, had a need to be reminded how much He was loved, cherished, and dear to the Father. Jesus had two friends, Mary and Martha. One day He was coming to visit, and they were both working like crazy to prepare. Once Jesus arrived, Mary sat down at Jesus' feet and listened. Martha kept right on working. Martha got irritated (oh, my, there's that irritability again), and Jesus' response to her was one I needed to hear. "Mary has chosen what is better, and it will not be taken away from her. (Luke 10:42)" Jesus knew what I needed to remember. If we skip our time with the One Who loves us unconditionally, we are opening ourselves up to being irritable. We begin trying to live life in our own strength. We begin aborting our "nice."

As I reflect upon some of the things which have been taking place in our country, I think perhaps it would do us all good to remember the importance of watering our relationship with the Father. Perhaps we will even need to extend our time spent in His presence. It can be a challenge to avoid getting caught up in the negativity and conflict stirring about these days. Don't forget that self-control was part of the fruit of the Spirit also (speaking to myself as much as anyone else). How about you? Are you finding yourself more on edge? Are you experiencing any agitation based upon your surroundings? How about fear? I've noticed he has been trying to sneak in the back door so he isn't as noticeable. If you find your mood shifting, ask yourself why? And take it as a good indicator God is just calling you back to spend more time with Him. He loves you so much He can't wait to hang out with you. Reassure you. Give you water so your fruit can ripen and feed others. There's nowhere else that is more peaceful and relaxing to be than right at the feet of Jesus. Why not go sit with Mary and hear what He has to say? And then invite someone else to do the same.

PLUG IN

There are days during the summer months which can be sweltering hot. We had some of those this summer. It was in the 90s with heat index warnings. Mind you, I'd take hot over cold any day of the week, but it created a bit of angst in our home. Abbie drives a red Ford pickup. And the air conditioner wasn't working. She took it to a dealer a couple years ago, and they put in a used air conditioner but told her they couldn't guarantee it would work. Guess what? Yep, lots of hot days! Thus, each time it was going to be above 80, we'd engage in this "discussion" as to whether she could take my vehicle to work. "Mom, what are your plans for the day?" "Mom, I have to drive two hours today, could I take your car?" I don't really know why it became a point of contention between us. It wasn't most days, but once we upgraded vehicles, I became a little more possessive. I don't know why. It is just a car, but a bit of selfishness, I suppose.

Well, John and I talked about it and decided maybe we would surprise her and get the air conditioner fixed. The pick-up needed to have the brakes checked, so John was going to ask the mechanic to check the air and give us an estimate on what it would cost. We knew big bucks would mean it wasn't going to happen, which is why she's been driving without it for so long. Yep, she received several of the "when we were kids" stories and was a wee bit tired of them to say the least.

John stopped yesterday to touch base with the mechanic while the truck was in the shop. He explained that there was a used air conditioner in the truck and wondered if there was a solution beyond a new one. We love our mechanic! He said, "Well, let me crawl under the truck and take a look before we order anything." GET READY! THIS IS HILARIOUS! Two years. No air. Driving in a hot box on 100-degree days. The. Air. Was. Not. Plugged. In. Yes, you heard correctly. The people who installed it failed to plug it in. It would have worked the entire time but wasn't hooked up.

Oh, you can see it coming, can't you? How often are we suffering? We're uncomfortable? We start whining because we're "hot." We walk around miserable when all we need to do is plug in to our source. We've got all we need. We've got Jesus, His Spirit, and the Word. The Holy Spirit will teach us and recharge us through the Word. But we need to plug in. It does us no good to drive around with our cord unplugged. Because, while we have the power to live in victory, if we don't plug into it, we're going to sit with Jesus but not be filled with all the fruits that the Spirit has to offer. We're in the truck. We're driving around. (aka we know Jesus and are believers) But we are still hot and miserable. Plug in! Let the Holy Spirit lead you, guide you, fill you, talk to you, direct you and bring you all the joy Jesus has to offer. BUT if you don't plug in to Him, if you drive around with your cord dangling, you're going to be miserable. Oh, you'll function, but not with the incredible joy God has intended. The journey with Jesus is meant to be full, not just functional.

"But you will receive power when the Holy Spirit comes on you; and you will be my witnesses in Jerusalem, and in all Judea and Samaria, and to the ends of the earth. (Acts 1:8)"

"But Saul, who was also called Paul, filled with the Holy Spirit, looked intently at him. (Acts 13:9)"

WHOSE REPORT

Someone made the comment this morning that they woke up, and their phone showed that it was snowing outside. They went to their window, and their eyes told them something different. Where they lived, it was not snowing. This brought to my mind the story of Joshua.

Moses and the Israelites came to the land of Canaan. God told Moses, "Send some men to explore the land of Canaan, which I am giving to the Israelites. (Numbers 13:2a)" Moses obeyed God and sent twelve men into the land to explore. When they came back to report to Moses, they reported a land fruitful and filled with milk and honey. "... Caleb silenced the people before Moses and said, 'We should go up and take possession of the land, for we can certainly do it. (Numbers 13:30) '" However, ten of the other men who had been on the expedition reported people in the land who were big and strong and spread a "bad report" among the people.

As a result of the bad report, people began complaining and grumbling. Joshua and Caleb told the people, "Only do not rebel against the Lord. And do not be afraid of the people of the land, because we will devour them. Their protection is gone, but the Lord is with us. Do not be afraid of them. (Numbers 14:9)" Unfortunately, there were people who did not trust God at this crucial point in time and instead the people ended up wandering in the wilderness for forty years. God still loved them. God walked with them even in the wilderness. But the journey through the wilderness was not necessary. It could have been avoided had the people chosen to believe the Lord rather than men. When I read Numbers 13:2a it struck me that God said he was **giving** them the land. They already knew it was theirs. But they did not step out in faith and take the gift He had promised.

We've been living in a year with a great deal of negative reports. March brought with it a tremendous amount of reporting about COVID-19. We followed that with the news full of rioting and violence. You don't need to go far to find arguing and anger. It's a great opportunity for fear to attempt to get a foothold. The ten spies could see that the land was filled with milk and honey but instead they focused on their fear of people. The report they gave was rooted in unbelief. A fear that the people of the land were stronger than the Lord. Has fear been trying to take root in your life? Are you looking at the evil in the world and feeling unsettled?

I just want to encourage you today to look to the cross. God proved His great love for us when He sent His one and only Son to die in our place. And better yet, rise again! He loves us. We can rejoice because He is **still** in control. It doesn't matter what your "phone" reports, and it doesn't matter what the news and/or social media is saying. What matters is where your eyes are focused, and who your heart is believing. If your eyes are looking to Jesus, you will see a great, big God. He wants His children to walk in obedience and faith. He wants us to trust His way in the best way. He will give His children the land. We have direct access to conversation with the Father each and every moment of every day. We can take the fear that is running rampant in the world directly to the Father in prayer. It doesn't need to be fancy. It just needs to be genuine. Your prayer will be perfect by the time it reaches God's ears. Where is your focus? Have you been taking your burdens and concerns to the Lord? Press on believers by going to your knees. Look to the Lord. Whose report will you believe? I will believe the report of the Lord!

"If my people, which are called by my name, shall humble themselves, and pray, and seek my face, and turn from their wicked ways; then will I hear from heaven, and will forgive their sin, and will heal their land. (2 Chronicles 7:14)"

LISTEN AND
OBEY

A bout two months ago, I was at preschool, and it was snack time. I bit into the snack of the day only to feel something give way in my tooth. I usually don't have trouble with my teeth, so this was somewhat new to me. I was digging and digging away in my teeth, and it didn't take long for little inquiring minds to begin asking me just exactly what I was doing? I told them I thought I had something stuck in my tooth, but the longer it went on, the more convinced I was that a filling had fallen out. So, off to the dentist I went.

I love my dentist, which makes a trip there not quite so scary. It's actually a chance to catch up on life except the instruments in my mouth always make it a bit challenging. Yep, it was a lost filling. AND a cracked tooth. The dentist filled my tooth with a new filling that day and suggested I come in for a crown **as soon as possible.** I left the dentist office without making an appointment. (I think this might be where I made my first mistake.)

I determined if my tooth felt good, why have it crowned? Right? After all, I HAVEN'T gone to school for dentistry and therefore have nothing to base this ever so brilliant decision upon. All was going well until a road trip one evening and a bite into my delicious

45

meal. UGH! Are you kidding me? Pain, pain, pain. Why does it feel like I have something stuck in the back of my teeth?

Well, back to the dentist I go. Only this time, I **was** experiencing angst. Am I going to get scolded for not coming in sooner, OR is it going to be nothing? Upon further examination, it appeared the crack definitely needed a crown. If the tooth started to throb, I may even need to see a specialist for a root canal.

Okay, really? We went from a lost filling to a root canal? I am thankful to say as I've waited for my crown appointment and made certain to chew on the other side of my mouth, that there has been no throbbing or pain. Until tonight. Oh, it doesn't hurt bad, but it's enough to make me aware that I still need that crown. (Just in case I had remotely toyed with the idea of cancelling my appointment.)

Is this how we are with Jesus? We feel that initial little pain. Hmm, what's the cause? Did someone look at us funny? Disagree with us at a meeting? Perhaps we're even in a church setting and someone else's sarcasm doesn't sit well. You know what we call it? It's when we get OFFENDED. Ouch. Pain. (Lost filling) We might even do the right thing and go to our Great Physician. He soothes our wounds and reminds us how much we are loved. He also tells us we need to forgive the offender and come back to see Him so our wound doesn't re-open. (You know, get the crown.) But we think since we're feeling good again that we don't need to take that next step. We can just kind of ignore it. Here's the crazy thing about hurt, though. It doesn't heal without being fixed. And sometimes getting restored to good health takes more than one trip to the throne of God.

If I had made my appointment for the crown immediately, I would not have been in the predicament of ruining my supper and needing to eat on one side of my mouth. But I didn't. My dentist fixed my tooth the first time; however, she was very clear there was a second step to fully fixing the problem. I just failed to listen.

When someone hurts us, when we experience the pain of a loss, when we've run to the Father, and He tells us to come back, it's important that we listen and obey. Ooohh, did we catch that part? Obey. It can be a difficult word to swallow sometimes, but it's an important one. You see, going back to the Father again reminds us again the importance of forgiveness. The value we have in His eyes. We are loved. (Isn't offended sometimes just another word for "I felt rejected?") We are chosen. We are forgiven. We are enough. Oh, yes, and then "... bless those who curse you... (Romans 12:14)" A great way to bless someone is through prayer. It will bring healing to your soul. If you let that pain go unattended, it will continue to flare up. It will continue to fester. And it will impact the rest of your life activities.

I encourage you, if you're dealing with pain today, go to Jesus. And, go again to Jesus. It's not a stop once to fix all. It's a continual relationship with a Savior who adores you. He wants the best for you. I can obey, BECAUSE I trust Him. I don't obey out of fear. I do it out of a heart of love and trust. If you're questioning whether He can be trusted with your pain...yep! Know how I know? Because He died for you and me. Let me say that again, He died for you and me! Wow! And He rose again! Now that's a love worth trusting.

Oh, and one more thought on this subject. Remember how my dentist said I could need a root canal? (Again, no throbbing so I feel certain we've dodged that bullet, or shall I say drill?) If we continue to ignore pain, guess what can happen? A root of bitterness can sneak in there. And bitterness is a nasty little sin that steals joy in a big hurry. God doesn't want us to have to carry around bitterness. "Make every effort to live in peace with all men and to be holy; without holiness no one will see the Lord. See to it that no one misses the grace of God and that no bitter root grows up to cause trouble and defile many. (Hebrews 12:14-15)" Trust Him. Go right away. Let His love bring healing. Walk in obedience. The Lord watches over those who obey him, those who trust in his constant love. (Psalm 33:18)

YOU BELONG
TO GOD

W e've seen a lot of changes in the past few months. I don't know about you, but I don't even listen to the news anymore. There are times I feel like I could burst from the negativity being spewed out. I sometimes feel like I need to put on my teacher's voice and remind everyone to "use your nice words." But you know what's amazing? In the midst of all unknowns, we have a God Who is crazy about us. Scripture is very clear. "But you belong to God, my dear children. You have already won a victory over those people, because the Spirit who lives in you is greater than the spirit who lives in the world. (1 John 4:4)"

We don't need to add to the problems. We don't need to join in the negativity. And we certainly don't need to walk in fear. Because if you know Jesus, you are God's child. We have an authority that comes from being sons and daughters of the Creator of the universe. He is not surprised by what is happening around us. He is not sitting in Heaven gasping with astonishment over the chaos He is seeing. Oh, I think He may be heartbroken and saddened, but not surprised. His hurt would come from making the sacrifice of giving His Son so people could know true love only to have them not see it. Not receive it. Not walk in His grace.

Really, we shouldn't be surprised. (Oh, don't get me wrong. I've been downright flabbergasted. In fact, I didn't even know I could be this shocked by people's behavior.) I mean, for heaven's sake, I can't even grasp what would make a person think that ruining someone else's property, showing disrespect, or calling names is going to solve a problem. And I'm not going to apologize for teaching my children to stand up during our national anthem! I thought some of these behaviors were innate. Built in. You just know there are lines you don't cross even in the heat of an argument. But then I realize that "The person without the Spirit does not accept the things that come from the Spirit of God but considers them foolishness and cannot understand them because they are discerned only through the Spirit. (1 Corinthians 2:14)" An unbeliever is not going to respond like a believer. They can't. They lack the Spirit of the Living God. God is alive. He's powerful. He's active. And He is living on the inside of you! IF you have allowed Him entrance.

I'd like to challenge everyone, myself included, before you do anything else, pray. Pray that God will give YOU the perspective you need to walk in faith. Pray for the salvation of those who don't know Him. And pray for the Spirit to fill you and empower you to walk in victory regardless of the circumstances around you.

"...if my people, who are called by my name, will humble themselves and pray and seek my face and turn from their wicked ways, then I will hear from heaven, and I will forgive their sin and will heal their land. (2 Chronicles 7:14)"

ON THOSE DAYS

S ome days, it just hurts. No matter how you look at it, it hurts. You have wants and needs, and no one seems to be able to even understand what they are. You need a hug, but the people closest don't want to or seem to know how to meet those needs. You're trying to express the pain inside. The loneliness. The need to be loved. But in their own pain they can't hear it. They hear control. They want to avoid. They run from your pain, because they don't want to see their own. They can't go there.

What do we do on the days where it all seems hopeless? Where the journey seems long, and the road we're on appears to be all uphill. The days we're crying out, but no one hears us. Or we're not willing to face the rejection that comes with being vulnerable. Where do we turn? How do we keep going?

It is that day. Lord, I'm crying out to you. Help me. Show me. Love me. Encourage me. May I be so full of your Holy Spirit that my need for love elsewhere is minimal. Reveal to me what to do with the hurt and the pain. Please water the fields with my tears so the harvest will be plentiful. There is much here.

Others quit. They turn away. They seek love elsewhere. Lord, I want to obey. I want to hear you. I want to know you. I yearn for unity. I yearn to be understood. I yearn for more of You, Jesus. More of You.

I will trust You, Jesus. I will seek You. I will not give up all the days of my life. If the journey seems hard, I will walk with You knowing You have a plan. I will find encouragement in Your Word. I will sing with Your angels. I will remain hopeful in Your promises. You are a good and gracious God, and You love me. Thank You forever. Thank You, Jesus.

"Come to me, all you who are weary and burdened, and I will give you rest. (Matthew 11:28)"

FRECKLES

John just stopped in the house while his truck was loading. As he headed out the door, he said, "Come on, Freckles." For years, wherever John has gone, the dog has gone.

It was so hard to watch as Freckles went through this dilemma. Should he follow John or stay on the deck with me? As Freckles has aged, following John has been much more difficult. He is slowing down and walking can cause him pain. Yet, he has a great love for John and didn't want to miss out either. As he looked over his shoulder at me, I told him he could go with John if he wanted. I didn't want him feeling guilty about leaving me if John was his person of choice. In the end, he decided to stay put on the deck. This day, the walk was just more than he was up for.

I wonder if this is how God feels as He watches us make choices every day. In Freckle's situation, both were good choices. But often our choices are between God's way or the world's way. Follow Him or follow sin. Follow the "new thing" He wants to do or remain complacent in the old. We always have a choice. Why is the choice so difficult at times? After all, God demonstrated His love for us is so deep that He gave His only Son for us. We know His way will always be for our best.

"But if serving the Lord seems undesirable to you, then choose for yourselves this day whom you will serve, whether the gods your ancestors served beyond the Euphrates, or the gods of the Amorites, in whose land you are living. But as for me and my household, we will serve the Lord. (Joshua 24:15)" I pray today that you choose Jesus.

HEIRS AND ROYALTY

"And if children, then heirs—heirs of God and fellow heirs with Christ, provided we suffer with him in order that we may also be glorified with him."

Romans 8:17

Did you catch that as you read verse 17 from Romans? You are an heir. And not just any heir, but an heir of God. God. Did you hear it, because I can say it a third time? If you have accepted Christ as your personal Savior, you are an heir to the God who created the heavens and the earth. Do you know what that makes you? Either a prince or a princess. How cool is that? I am a princess of the King of Kings. You, sister, are a princess of the King of Kings. If you're not a girl, obviously, you are a prince of the King of Kings.

Yesterday, I was with a friend of mine who was struggling with discouragement. As we sat together in our little group of royalty, we began to pray. I wish you could have been there to join us. Why? Two reasons. First, there is nothing better than going to the throne of the Father Who loves us. He is amazing and always ready to allow us to climb into His lap and hold us while He reassures us through His Word. Second, as this sister of mine began to pray, she began to gain momentum. Her voice became stronger. Her spirit was renewed. You could hear it in her voice that the fire was back. I started giggling during prayer and told her, "I think the princess found her sword!"

You see, we were not left on this earth without a weapon. God loves us and His Spirit lives in us. You have a gift. You have the gift of a Savior. You have the gift of a Bridegroom. You have the gift of salvation. You have a Dad who owns the cattle on a thousand hills. You have the Holy Spirit, and you have the armor of God.

"Finally, be strong in the Lord and in his mighty power. Put on the full armor of God, so that you can take your stand against the devil's schemes. For our struggle is not against flesh and blood, but against the rulers, against the authorities, against the powers of this dark world and against the spiritual forces of evil in the heavenly realms. Therefore, put on the full armor of God, so that when the day of evil comes, you may be able to stand your ground, and after you have done everything, to stand. Stand firm then, with the belt of truth buckled around your waist, with the breastplate of righteousness in place, and with your feet fitted with the readiness that comes from the gospel of peace. In addition to all this, take up the shield of faith, with which you can extinguish all the flaming arrows of the evil one. Take the helmet of salvation and the sword of the Spirit, which is the word of God. And pray in the Spirit on all occasions with all kinds of prayers and requests. With this in mind, be alert and always keep on praying for all the Lord's people. (Ephesians 6:10-18)"

Friends, don't give in to discouragement right now. Don't lose your focus. Don't take your eyes off the Savior. You are a princess/prince and a daughter/son of the King of Kings. Put on your armor, pick up your sword, and keep praying. He is there. We only need to listen and be filled. Be still and know that He is God!

WALLS OF JERICHO

"Jesus entered Jericho and was passing through."
Luke 19:1

This Scripture has grabbed my attention in a way few others have for a while. I read it in church on Sunday and haven't been able to let it go. Something about the fact that Jesus entered Jericho was fascinating to me.

Jericho was a walled city and the first city the Israelites came to when they entered the Promised Land. The Lord met Joshua and told him exactly what he needed to do in order to gain victory over the town. He was to march around the city one time each day for seven days, and on the seventh day they were to march around seven times. On the seventh time when the priests blew their horns with a long blow, everyone was to yell. It was at this point that the walls crumbled to the ground, and the Israelites took control of the city. Joshua 6

Joshua 6 is fascinating, and I would encourage you to read it. I would actually begin at the beginning of the book to gain a bit more information. It was the walls that struck me as a point of interest between Joshua and Jericho. You see, Joshua and the Israelites were obedient and followed God's directions. As a result, God knocked the walls around the city down and gave the Israelites possession of the town.

The very same town that Jesus entered and was passing through. Remember, there is a significant time span between these two events. I haven't done the research to see when Jericho was rebuilt. Joshua placed a curse on anyone who attempted to rebuild it. But someone must have rebuilt it, because Jesus entered it. And when He entered, He walked right up to Zaccheus (remember, he was a short man who had climbed the tree to see Jesus) and invited Himself over to Zaccheus' house. Zaccheus was ecstatic! He welcomed Jesus into his home and into his heart. He immediately changed who he was and how he did business. Jesus does that to people. (Luke 19:1-10)

Here's the thing I find fascinating and incredibly symbolic. It was Joshua's obedience that God used to bring down those walls. And, as a result, they were already down when Jesus arrived. He walked up to Zaccheus and extended the invitation to welcome Him into his home. Whoa!

Can you see it? Oh, my goodness! It makes me want to be obedient. Think about the walls you have built in your life. I hope you don't have any, but if you do, are you willing to be obedient and let God tear them down? He can and will do it. But He's waiting for you to be willing. It can be hard to make changes. Responding in an unhealthy way may be the only way you know. But God is in the business of transforming lives. His love is like that. It envelops us and fills all those holes we've been trying to wall off. How did He do it with the Israelites? He asked them to be obedient. They didn't obey just one day either. It was seven days in a row. Their act of obedience could have looked silly if you didn't know what they were doing.

Opinions of others was not their motivation. Trusting their Father was!

Jump ahead how many years later, and the walls were down when Jesus entered. Would you be more willing to surrender those walls if you knew removing them would open the door for someone to meet Jesus? I know I'm viewing this from a symbolic standpoint, but it's one worth considering. Because if God wants to use me or you to reach people, let's be willing. Eternity is a very long time. Walking with Jesus is the difference between a life of joy, peace, and love versus one separated from the Savior.

Trust Him today to take down your walls. Ask Him what the walls are? When do they go up? I discovered the other day that if I think someone is angry with me, my walls are up immediately. I was sharing this little discovery with John and his response was, "Yeah, I know that."

I asked, "How long have you known this?" Well, apparently, he had been aware of it for a long time. I asked why he hadn't mentioned it sooner, and he laughed. A lot. Apparently, he felt that was dangerous ground, and he wasn't stepping into a potential fire storm.

Oh, I want that wall removed. Sometimes people aren't really angry. I don't want to be flipping walls up around my heart for no reason. It's just an unhealthy defense mechanism to avoid getting hurt. There's no need to close off communication. Rather, I want to keep my door of communication open. I want to hear what the other person is saying, share my own feelings, and achieve resolution. I can't control their anger, but I can control how I respond to anger whether real or perceived.

It's a wall. It has some unhealthy characteristics. I will trust and obey when God asks me to respond differently. Wouldn't it be amazing if its removal opens the door for someone else to see Jesus? I don't know if that will happen. But if there's even a chance that change would bring about the opportunity for someone else to meet Jesus, I'm willing. It won't be easy, but I'm willing. Are you?

DEVELOPING AS
A BELIEVER

O ne of the things I love to do in the mornings, especially before I go to school, is to sit down and read my Bible while I have breakfast. God is gracious and meets me at the kitchen counter or table each and every time. This morning, I came to sit with my yogurt and noticed instead of my Bible, my Early Childhood Development book was resting beside the computer. Oy! I'd have a lot more homework completed if I had stuck with it last night instead of getting hooked on that Hallmark series with subtitles.

It's actually fascinating learning about how children develop. I won't go into all the details, because if you're not into that type of thing, it would likely not get your blood pumping the way it does mine. However, there is a basic fundamental insight I will share. A child has to be developmentally ready to learn something before they're going to really get it. You've likely watched it happen at some time or another with someone you know. You see their eyes light up (FYI those are some of a teacher's FAVORITE moments,) and it's full steam ahead.

But what surfaced in my mind this morning is how very much like the children we are. "And I will be a father to you, and you shall be sons and daughters to Me, says the Lord Almighty. (2 Corinthians 6:18)" You see, we are God's children. And, "I gave you milk, not solid food, for you were not yet ready for it. Indeed, you are still not ready. (1 Corinthians 3:2)" And we are also each developing at our own rate. How often have you wondered why you just can't "get it together" in a certain area of your life? Or, worse yet, how often have we looked at someone else and wondered why they weren't finding victory in an area. Is it possible they just aren't ready yet? Are they still babes, and if they were given adult food, it could cause more harm than good?

God's Spirit is for everyone. Walking and living in victory is for everyone. But, let's face it, life is full of challenges. Sometimes what appears to be a bruise to someone's spirit from our perspective can actually be a near fatal blow from theirs. We want to get in the habit of lifting each other up. "When I bring the sword against a land, and the people of the land choose one of their men and make him their watchman, and he sees the sword coming against the land and blows the trumpet to warn the people… (Ezekiel 33:2b-3)" You may be someone's watchman, and your job is to see the sword coming and alert the others. If we're busy passing judgement or criticizing their behavior, is it possible we didn't blow the trumpet and alert others to go to battle on their behalf? The person we're fussing about may not be developmentally ready per se. They might still be drinking milk spiritually. We wouldn't expect a child to engage in a battle. We'd anticipate the physically mature and developed would engage. Is it time for us to stop trying to figure out "why someone isn't doing something" and instead stand in the gap for them? It may be an area God has grown you and set you free. You may be the very person needed to finish their walk into victory. You may be the one to assist them in standing before the throne and experiencing their "aha" moment with Jesus.

Ask yourself today, am I still a babe somewhere in my spiritual walk? Where might I need to unpack and let God start healing?

Where might He be issuing the challenge of 1 Corinthians 13:11? "When I was a child, I talked like a child, I thought like a child, I reasoned like a child. When I became a man, I put the ways of childhood behind me." We are living in a world that needs spiritually fit warriors. Are you willing to pick up your sword and your shield? Are you willing to let God develop you so you're ready to eat meat rather than the milk of babes? It may not be easy. Unpacking can be hard. Surrendering feels against the culture. But God is calling us to an intimate and glorious walk with Him. He wants us to continue to develop and grow. He yearns for us to come to Him. Whether you're in a season of rest and healing, growth and development, or have been placed on the wall as the watchman, I encourage you to seek Jesus. "For those who are led by the Spirit of God are the children of God. (Romans 8:1)"

THE CONCH
SHELL

I f you don't know what a conch shell is, don't feel bad. We had a local native Floridian tell us what it was and how to pronounce it. And then I had to google how to actually spell it. I'm going to attach a picture because I have a handful of devotions I'd like to share about this crazy gift God dropped in my (our) laps.

If you vacation with our family, be forewarned that we don't just lay around all day. We are up some mornings by 5:00 or 5:30 to go shelling. It's interesting to see who wants to find what. John loves to hunt for sand dollars which are still intact (not alive). The girls like the sand dollars, but they're like me in wanting to discover something of size. You see those big, beautiful seashells in the movies, and that's what we decided we wanted to find this time. If you want to make a discovery like that, you might need to be first on the beach!

On this particular day, I was lagging a bit behind. John and the rest of the crew had already reached the point of the island. I was walking in the water (because, of course, that's where all the good shells are, right?) and noticed something out a few steps from shore. My heart started pounding as soon as I saw it, because if this was a shell, it was gigantic! I went to have a look and ever so wisely poked it with my toe to be sure it was safe to touch. I picked it up, and it was the BIGGEST shell I had ever held! As you will notice by the picture, it isn't very attractive. But I didn't care, because it was huge! I immediately said, "Oh, Lord, You must really love me to give me this one!" I grabbed that thing with a smile a mile wide and headed to find the gang. I couldn't wait to show them!

As I approached my crew with my treasure in tow, I heard one of the girls say, "That's the shell I saw!" And instead of rounds of cheering over my big find, they're all talking at once concurring that she had, in fact, seen the shell first. I finally responded, "Well, I am the one who went and got it." I then followed that up with the ever-so-logical question, "Why didn't you go get it when you saw it?"

I'm not throwing anyone under the bus here, but her response was one that in our spiritual lives is very sobering. She said, "I was told it was a coconut." And she proceeded to let the false report of those with her sway what she knew in her heart to be true. She let their false assessment of the situation determine her actions. Thus, the treasure was left for someone else (in this case me) to find.

Have you ever heard the Lord tell you something and let others convince you it wasn't His voice? Has He given you a vision for ministry, but since others couldn't see it, you set it aside? How often do we see an incredible gift God has for us and instead of reaching out and picking it up (let's face it, we might need to get our feet wet as we receive it), we convince ourselves it isn't really what we think it is? Do we possess a mindset that believes God has good gifts for us? Are you willing to grab hold of the gift (after a little kick to make sure it doesn't bite) and let your spirit shout, "Thank You for loving me with this God!" Or do we allow the world's perspective to cloud our judgment?

We are living in a time where there is a lot of noise. It's not often that you can even sit in a room and hear nothing at all. It requires an intentional decision to step away from the noise and listen to the Lord. And as you take time to be with Him, He will show you His will. His desires. The gifts He has for you. But just as when the spies headed into the Promised Land, twelve were sent and only two believed God would give them the gift He had shown them (Numbers 13). As a result of the unbelief of the ten, the Israelites spent forty years wandering around the wilderness.

We get to choose who we listen to also. Will you trust the voice of God and embrace the gifts He has for you? Will you view your life circumstances through His eyes, or will you have the vision of the world? As you go deeper with Jesus, it will require learning to lean in and trust His voice. His heart. His desire to give you good gifts (James 1:17). Those around you might truly see a "coconut" when you see "a huge shell." God may not be giving them the same vision for the same situation. It may not be their time. But don't allow someone else's inability to see deter you from the course God has set out before you. Get out there and grab it. Embrace it. Rejoice that He loves you so much He was willing to bless you with good and perfect gifts. "The thief comes only to steal and kill and destroy; I have come that they may have life and have it to the full. (John 10:10 [NIV])" Choose life. Choose joy! Choose His way, because it's His best for you!

(The shell was returned to the water alive and intact.)

THE CONCH SHELL: PART II

Yesterday, I shared about the big conch shell we found on vacation. I couldn't just leave the story where I did, because that shell has caused me a lot of angst. As you could see by the picture I posted yesterday, I took the shell back to the house with me and tried to determine what to do with it. How was I supposed to clean it? And what about the conch inside? After some discussion, I decided to put it outside in the event of a death. Let's face it, no one wanted to smell rotten marine life for the rest of vacation.

We went about our day and would occasionally go and check on the shell. I was carrying around a tremendous amount of guilt. There was not (and is not) a doubt in my mind that God gave me that shell. I needed it. I needed the reassurance of His presence and power, and that shell was His earthly sign to me at that moment. However, I was wrestling with the idea of what lived inside the shell. I didn't want something to die for no reason. Was it really worth it for me to have this pretty (or not so pretty) shell on my shelf? (Have I ever mentioned I can be an overthinker?) I wrestled with it all day. Later that evening, John and I were sitting outside, and he poked the "creature" inside the shell. It was still alive. Ugh. We decided right then and there to return it to the water. We took a picture and set it free.

Oh, ya, we sound like heroes, don't we? Ha! No. Oh, my word. I have no idea how my husband hunts! No hero here (except maybe my husband). Do you want to know what my biggest struggles have been? I didn't want to disappoint God. He gave me this great big, beautiful shell, and I threw it back! I threw it back. He gave me a desire of my heart (Psalm 37:4), and I felt weak for not wanting to keep it. Friends, the struggle is real. (Did I mention it takes 10-20 years for this particular specimen to grow to the full size of 8 inches? Our gigantic shell was likely close to the 16 inches, which offshore whelks can reach.)

The lessons I have learned from this shell have been endless. (Oh, today's lesson is not the last from the shell.) I knew that shell was a gift from God. I knew what He was saying and why it was there. And I embraced it. I received it. I was excited about it and shared that excitement and joy with others. I took the gift He had given home with me. I enjoyed it and was even wise where the gift was placed. It leads one to ask the question, what gift is God placing in front of you today? Can you see it? Do you want it? Are you willing to receive it? Will you share it with others? The bigger question I have for you, will you cherish those gifts He has given you, or will you toss them aside as if it isn't a gift at all?

Shall I be direct? What about your marriage? Do you remember your spouse is one of God's greatest gifts in your life? Do you treat him/her like the treasure they are? (I hope you don't set them outside, because they're starting to stink.) Or have you tossed them aside and in essence told God that you don't value who He has given you? What about your children? They are a treasure to be cherished. Your relationships? Health? Employment? The list of God's amazing gifts are endless and well worth seeking out. If you hunt for them with the same fervor of a sheller, you'll see them everywhere. "You will seek Me and find Me when you seek Me with all your heart. (Jeremiah 29:13)" God is the Giver of good and perfect gifts. Whether you hold them for a season or a lifetime, they are to be enjoyed and embraced. And I'm learning, when it's time to return the gift to the Giver, don't stress over it. Trust Him. It may be giving life to something or someone else.

And, finally, I was not willing to let something die in order to keep the gift. I'm not sure there was a right or wrong in this situation. However, it's worth noting that often if we want to be closer to the Lord and embrace all He has for us, there may be parts of us which will need to die. Romans 6:8 says, "Now if we died with Christ, we believe that we will also live with him." The dying process of old habits and sins which may try to hold us can be painful to walk through, yet as we rise in Christ and experience more of His love and acceptance, we have the joy of knowing an unconditional love which changes and refines us.

Therefore, if anyone is in Christ, the new creation has come: The old has gone, the new is here! (2 Corinthians 5:17)

MORE OF HIM

Today will be the last day involving conchs, unless God leads me otherwise, of course. The day after we threw the large conch back into the gulf, we had rented a boat for an afternoon. We had a great guy (his name really was Guy) who took us to other islands and sandbars in the gulf to go shelling. As we were explaining the types of shells we were hoping to find, I pulled up the picture on my phone and showed him our big shell. He was incredibly helpful and full of information.

Guy told us that the shell was a conch. Apparently, the discovery was very rare because they had pretty much disappeared after the red tide. He said they were just beginning to see them again and indicated where ours had been found was quite unusual. Then he began to explain what to do in order to eat them. He told us when a conch is found, you can put it in boiling water to cook it, explained how to pop the conch out of the inside, and ways of preparing the food. I guess this is a food he really enjoys eating. He then proceeded to fill us in on the process of saving the shell after the conch inside had been eaten. He said if you soak the shell in bleach water and use a toothbrush, you are able to scrub off the unattractive color and expose the beauty of the shell before it's been tarnished by its surroundings.

Now wouldn't that have been helpful information 24 hours ago?! Well, we stored that tidbit of new information and went about our afternoon. We enjoyed each location he took us to and learned so much about his childhood and how things in his environment had changed. As we came to one of the sandbars off the island, I pointed and yelled, "Look, is that a big shell?" John hardly waited for the boat to stop! He was out of the boat with his shell digger (FYI: GREAT Christmas gift) and scooped up a good-sized... you guessed it, conch! And glory to Jesus, we found about seven! Our guide couldn't believe it, because he said there just hadn't been any after the red tide. They'd only just begun to see a few again. The fact that we had found seven (no, we didn't keep them all) was amazing. We were allowed to keep one per person according to the guidelines of the county. And since we now knew what to do with them, it was decided we'd give it a try. Our guide was quite enthused and nabbed one for himself to take home and eat!

There were so many lessons for us on this outing. First, it was very interesting to have a guide with knowledge of the area. He grew up on the island. He knew what was what and had information not everyone would. I had thought to myself as he was sharing about the first conch we found, "Well, I wish we had had that information yesterday!" But, we hadn't. Hosea 4:6 says, "My people are destroyed for lack of knowledge..." As I continue to grow in my walk with the Lord, I am sobered by how much I don't know. I want all of Him. I sometimes feel like I am standing next to an iceberg, and as one chunk is chipped off, and God reveals a new part of Himself, I get all excited and humbled. Then, I look up to see this giant, massive glacier that is still untouched. We're on a journey with the Lord. It will take us an eternity to know Him. But we are so blessed to discover a little more each day. (Just for the record, God is not cold like an iceberg.) If we're destroyed for lack of knowledge, we need to pursue knowledge and a relationship with Jesus like our very soul depends upon it. Because, in reality, it does.

The process of cooking and cleaning the conch also spoke to me. How often do we meet people, ourselves included, who are covered in gunk. The world has discolored the very person God has created them to be. We need to be prepared for the cooking and cleaning process. There may be times God will allow us to be tested. "...so that the tested genuineness of your faith—more precious than gold that perishes though it is tested by fire—may be found to result in

praise and glory and honor at the revelation of Jesus Christ." 1 Peter 1:7 In order to find the beauty of the shell, it had to first be boiled. Personally, I wish there was a way to get rid of the unbelief and grow faith without trials. "I have told you these things, so that in me you may have peace. In this world you will have trouble. But take heart! I have overcome the world." John 16:33 We live in a world, however, where God forewarned us that trials and troubles would come. We can rejoice that those trials, while challenging, will not defeat us. God promises He has overcome the world. And through the process, He will gently scrub away at our discoloration and reveal more and more of the person He truly created us to be.

The picture above shows you I attempted to polish one shell. I am not finished but wanted to experiment a bit. It made the color stand out that much more. It reminded me that even once God has the gunk off, we will continue to be polished to reveal more of Him in us. The very purpose for our existence is to walk in relationship with Jesus and glorify Him. The more of us He has, the more of Him that will be revealed. I pray that each day we will all surrender more of ourselves to the Savior. "Now to him who is able to do far more abundantly than all that we ask or think, according to the power at work within us, to him be glory in the church and in Christ Jesus throughout all generations, forever and ever. Amen. (Ephesians 3:20-21)"

THE SEA GULL

We love the beach, and when we have the opportunity to go, it is a common occurrence to rise early and walk the beach for shells. There are few things better than to feel the sand between your toes, smell the salt air, and feel you are on a treasure hunt for the perfect prize. Recently, as we were out on one of our morning walks, we noticed a group of seagulls. They are a fascinating species of birds to watch and on this particular day, they'd all congregated on the beach together.

As we were standing there watching, John drew my attention to one bird in particular. The bird was part of the group and appeared to be eating. However, as I watched it, I could see why John was pointing it out. It was missing a leg. I observed the bird for a while and what struck me the most was that even though it had a rather significant injury, it was still able to fly. It may not have won a race on the ground, but in the air no one would have even noticed it's lack of a limb. (Do you call bird's legs limbs?)

Upon reflection, you can likely guess where I'm going to go with this, can't you? We live in a world where we will receive injuries. John 16:33 tells us, "In this world you will have trouble…" Your injury may not be a missing limb. Do you know what it is? Have you lost someone you love? Perhaps you were offended by something someone said? Or what about that job you didn't get because you didn't have the right connections? Or worse yet, you were part of downsizing and are carrying the rejection? Have you allowed someone else to determine your self worth? Has someone tried to steal your dreams, and you've allowed it? Injuries don't always include a physical incapacity which is evident to the human eye. You can fill in your own blank as I'm sure you've experienced something. And I'm going to guess you know someone in your life carrying around an injury as well.

The hope we have comes in the last part of John 16:33 when God says, "But take heart! I have overcome the world." We don't need to become immobilized by our injuries. They do not get to define us. Just like the injured seagull, our worth is not dependent upon our injuries. There is no one who gets to choose our limitations except for our Savior. And He tells us that He has overcome the world. Since He has graciously chosen to take up residence inside our heart, we get to live in victory and freedom. ".. but those who hope in the LORD will renew their strength. They will soar on wings like eagles; they will run and not grow weary; they will walk and not be faint. (Isaiah 40:13)" Don't let the pain of this world determine the course of your life. Friend, you can still fly! I encourage you today to surrender the pain you're carrying. Open the grip of your fingers on those injuries and deliver them to the One who can do something with them. He has not called you to live in bondage to past (or current) wounds, but rather He will take them and use them for His glory. There is freedom and victory in the surrender. "...We walk by faith, not by sight. (2 Corinthians 5:7)" Grab hold of His hand, trust His heart, surrender your pain, and fly! You can be the leader your friends are searching for and the hope the world so desperately needs. Please, I pray you will take your pain and give it to the Great Physician. He is waiting for the moment you will release yourself from the hold it has had on you and soar again. You'll find the joy of the flight is light when you are no longer weighed down by the worries of this world.

THE EAGLE

There are few things more calming and joy-filled to my spirit than time spent at the ocean and the lake. There is just something about the sound of the waves that can remove the anxieties of the world and restore hope and faith. Today as we sat on the dock (lake) enjoying the sunshine, we heard the most interesting bird sound. I can't recall ever hearing it before, and it almost seemed that it was making noise to catch our attention. As we looked around to see what was making the noise, we spotted an eagle perched on the top of a nearby tree. It didn't move other than to turn its head from time to time. There was enough of a wind that I suspect he was enjoying all the joys of the lake which we were only from a much better view. We sat with our cameras ready hoping to catch a picture of him as he launched from the treetop. My daughter caught the best pictures, because I was too excited when he took off to do much clicking! He soared above us for a while before he took flight along the shoreline. I don't know if he was looking for food or just out enjoying the day. Regardless of his motivation, he brought an awe and a reverence to the morning which was greatly appreciated.

I think the amazing thing about eagles is their sense of power. I've never seen an eagle work hard to flap its wings. They catch the current of the wind and float and soar. If they get hungry, they can dive into the water at amazing speed and come out with a fish. It seems every move they make is peaceful and strong. Part of their presence seems to stem from the fact that they know their strength and rest in the assurance of it. Do you know we carry this same ability in Christ? We, too, have power and authority, because we are children of the King of Kings. According to Acts 2:2-4, "And suddenly there came a sound from heaven as of a rushing mighty wind, and it filled all the house where they were sitting. And there appeared unto them cloven tongues like as of fire, and it sat upon each of them. And they were all filled with the Holy Ghost, and began to speak with other tongues, as the Spirit gave them utterance."

We have been empowered through the Holy Spirit to walk in our authority in Christ. Just as the eagle soars on the wind currents, we can rest in the Spirit of God. We don't need to strive to make things happen but instead rest in Him to lead, guide, and empower. "The Spirit of the Sovereign Lord is on me, because the Lord has anointed me to proclaim good news to the poor. He has sent me to bind up the brokenhearted, to proclaim freedom for the captives and release from darkness for the prisoners. (Isaiah 61:1)" You have been chosen by God as an instrument to be used to help set others free. You can be part of their healing and direct them to the One who has set them free. I pray that you are walking in the freedom and victory God has intended for you. I pray that you are soaring in His Spirit and walking in the authority and confidence of who you are in Christ. You are a loved child of the Creator of the universe. He who spoke the world into existence loves YOU so much that He sent His one and only Son to die for you. And once you have received His gift of salvation, He wants you to experience and walk into the freedom that comes with it. Today is a great day to walk in faith. It is a great day to be filled with the Spirit of God and begin to walk in the joy of knowing and believing Him. He's where your freedom truly comes from. Grab hold! It's a great day to soar!

THE SQUADRON

Yesterday I shared about the eagle sitting in the tree who took flight and soared above us with ease. Tonight, God was gracious to demonstrate something I've not seen in 53 years of coming to this lake. We first saw one eagle (yes, we've seen that before). We then saw two eagles (once in a while we get to see two at a time). Of course, God didn't stop with two eagles, He then sent a third. (Okay, we've maybe seen this on a rare occasion when there has been a baby eagle.) No, we weren't done yet. As four eagles soared high above the far end of the lake, we watched in amazement. Each eagle was effortless as they soared. All were at different heights and all just gliding on the wind currents. But what amazed me the most was before it was done, we counted eight eagles all soaring together. We didn't see any eagles fighting for position or leadership. No, instead we witnessed all of them rising and soaring together.

I told Abbie it looked like a squadron of fighter planes. All were gliding and floating, just out for an evening flight. (We suspect there was a dead fish somewhere, but we didn't get close enough to confirm.) God brought several things to my mind as we witnessed this majestic event. First, it's amazing that as you begin to walk, surrendering more and more of your life to the Holy Spirit, you will find the peace that comes with "going higher." And as you soar higher, you will find God sending other believers to soar with you. Just as each eagle was at their own height in the sky (I was astounded how very high they were), they were all free. It will be no different for you and the fellow believers on this journey of faith with you. God has called you each to something different, yet you are all called and empowered to walk in victory. It doesn't matter who is higher or lower. It matters that you are walking in the freedom and joy God has called you. There may be days when the challenges have you closer to the ground, but you are still surrounded by the support system God has given you. There will be other times when you are walking filled with the Spirit, and God teaches you to go higher. He will enable you to see the battles surrounding you while allowing you to operate apart from them. "For our struggle is not against flesh and blood, but against the rulers, against the authorities, against the powers of this dark world and against the spiritual forces of evil in the heavenly realms. (Ephesians 6:12)" It is very possible to discern the warfare around you, engage in the battle, yet not become entangled in the distraction it could bring.

Seeing the "squadron" of eagles soaring together, it reminded me of the power a group of fellow worshipers can have together. There is a great song called War Cry by Henry Seely. It's amazing! We all have a war cry, and it is in the praise we offer up to Him Who sits upon the throne. As we saw those eagles all together, I felt myself rejoicing over the joy of being with other believers who are walking filled with God's Spirit and a desire to know Jesus more. To see one eagle in his majestic state is a moment of wonder, but there are barely words to describe the breath-holding awe of watching eight of these majestic birds soaring together. Can you envision what takes place in the heavens when God's fellow worshipers come together? God's children who love Him and adore Him. God's children who know the gift they've been given and choose to believe what He says about them. God's children who have accepted His gift of salvation and sonship. We are heirs to the kingdom of God. We are sons and daughters of the King. The more we walk in that Truth, the more we will soar like the eagles. And the more we soar together, the more impact we will have to influence this world for the next. "We are here for only a moment, visitors and strangers in the land as our ancestors were before us. Our days on earth are like a passing shadow, gone so soon without a trace. (1 Chronicles 29:15)" We may be visitors in this world, but we are heirs to the kingdom of God. (Romans 8:17) It's time to rise up and live like we are the royalty God has designed us to be. We are not intended to live in defeat. We are created with a purpose and are blessed to glorify God for His incredible gift of His Son Jesus. Let's soar. Let's worship. Let's impact the world around us before God calls us home!

CALL DAD

As I reflect upon the week we've spent at the lake in northern Minnesota, I can't help but think of the huge gamut of weather we've seen. We spent our first day in 80 degrees enjoying peace and calm in the boat with hardly a ripple on the water. We just floated along while Abbie fished, and I read a book. What a shock to our system when it was followed with a day of strong winds, whitecaps, cloudy weather, and a high in the 50s. We had to put on every stitch of warm clothing we had including our life jackets. We saw nights in the 30s where the morning weather screamed, "Stay inside! It's too cold to come out here!" (I was thankful on those mornings for indoor plumbing versus the outhouse of many years!) Yet, even the cold days were followed by bright sunshine, birds singing, and eagles effortlessly soaring above the lake.

One of those days on the water we anchored the boat to do some pan fishing. It was a sunny but fairly windy day. It was a great idea until we went to pull the anchor, the motor flooded, and discovered we had to paddle our way back to shore. (Into the wind, nonetheless!) Well, we arrived back at the dock sweaty, irritable, and relieved. Hmmm, two women and limited knowledge of motors. Abbie did what every wise woman does in this situation. She called her dad! John walked her through the steps to start the motor without flooding it, and the motor started right up! (We really should have tried the phone call BEFORE we paddled to shore. Did I mention it was into the wind with two paddles that didn't match? Oh, and she didn't mention this until much later, but the trolling motor was running in reverse the whole time we were paddling.)

Life in America has seen its own "gamut of weather" lately. It's interesting how one day we're sending the kids to school and going to work and next almost everything is closed, and the country is brought to an abrupt halt. Finally, everything begins to open back up, and we are met with riots, anger, and unrest. It's in moments like this I am ever so thankful for a God Who is unchanging. Isn't it wonderful that… "those who hope in the Lord will renew their strength. They will soar on wings like eagles; they will run and not grow weary; they will walk and not be faint. (Isaiah 40:31)" We don't have to panic. We don't have to be afraid. What did Abbie do when we needed help with the motor? She called her dad. We need be no different. Are you feeling the bite of the storm today? Does the shore seem like it's a long way off, and you're paddling against the wind? Are you experiencing fear? Loss? Unrest? You have a Dad Who is available and waiting. He wants to hear from you! "I called to the LORD, who is worthy of praise, and I have been saved from my enemies." Psalm 18:3 He will pour out His love for you and guide and direct your next step. He may ask you to pray about the situation. He may sit with you and reassure you. He may remind you He's got life under control. And He will most definitely walk beside you regardless of what comes your way. You can find peace in the storm, because God is in the storm with you. He has promised to never leave you or forsake you. "Where shall I go from your Spirit? Or where shall I flee from your presence? If I ascend to heaven, you are there! If I make my bed in Sheol, you are there! If I take the wings of the morning and dwell in the uttermost parts of the sea, even there your hand shall lead me, and your right hand shall hold me. (Psalm 139)" Regardless, whether you are soaring today in bright sunshine or paddling into the storm, God would love to spend time with you. I'd encourage you to give Him a call!

"If my people, which are called by my name, shall humble themselves, and pray, and seek my face, and turn from their wicked ways; then will I hear from heaven, and will forgive their sin, and will heal their land. (2 Chronicles 7:14)"

KISSED BY THE KING

The last day of vacation in northern Minnesota is always a somber event. As much as I begin missing home, there is something about sitting outside in the morning listening to the loons sing and watching the deer in the pasture that brings a peace to my soul like no other location has ever offered.

It is a rare week spent up north where flannel shirts and rubber shoes aren't a morning necessity. There is a joy found in sitting beside the glass lake early in the morning even when sweatshirts and jackets may be required to avoid the chill. The solitude of the northwoods is a perfect location to hear God speak without the distractions of the washing machine and daily responsibilities running through my mind.

There are times during the school year (especially when the classroom is abuzz with activity) when I'll stop and close my eyes. The children will inevitably also stop and ask, "What are you doing?" I respond with a simple, "I'm sitting by the lake in northern Minnesota for just a moment." It's my happy place. I can go there in my mind if needed and experience it.

Of course, I don't often remember during those moments the times when my brother locked me in the outhouse. Or the day I was crying because I had leeches stuck to my toes. Or even the night mom and dad were fishing, and I took the broom and tried to hit my brothers across the table in the cabin and knocked out the electricity. (In my own defense, a girl can only take so much of two brothers before she breaks.)

No, I remember the love of swimming across the lake with my dad. The feeling that I could accomplish anything with him by my side. (Rest assured, life jackets were worn by all.) Or hanging with my cousins for an entire week uninterrupted. As we've grown, I can feel in my heart the joy of watching our daughters play with their cousins. Annie Annie Over was a great game with the size of the cabins, hunting for shells, discovering schools of fish swimming by the shore, catching a huge walleye, or even losing a big one right next to the boat.

Closing my eyes doesn't typically bring any of those specific memories to my mind. However, as I close them and see the water, the emotions I feel are a result of years of memories created with those I love. It is the knowledge that even today those people love me, are loved by me, and understand the shared experience of life together.

Doing life together is part of knowing Jesus. As we build relationships, invest time into one another, and walk through the ups and downs, it creates a place of peace in our souls. A happy place. A place we can close our eyes and go when we need to remember we are loved. Whether our journey involves just one other person, or we're designed to be surrounded by many, we're so blessed to share it with others.

Jesus wants to be part of that. He is love. He wants to be part of the Annie Annie Over games. He wants to share the deer in the pasture. He's available to talk with, walk with, and do life with. In the midst of catching the big fish, thank Him. In the moment of fear in the outhouse, tell Him. The joy in hanging out with family for a week, He's there and part of it. He instigated it. He designed it. He even knows the frustrations involved with it. And, because He wants a relationship with us, He knows there will be times when we enjoy Him, laugh with Him, get angry with Him, and even need to forgive Him. He's not surprised by us. He created us. He wants all of us. He wants our hearts, our souls, our hurts, our raw emotions. He wants the real us. Raw, broken, vulnerable, overjoyed, or angry. Bring it to Him. As time progresses and the journey lengthens, you'll be able to close your eyes in the midst of a busy day and go to your happy place with your Savior. It may just take a moment. A moment to pause and allow your heart to be filled with the memories of His provision, peace, love, and joy. It's the filling of His eternal love and acceptance. It's in that moment, you will be ever so gently "Kissed by King."

"As a deer longs for a stream of cool water, so I long for you, O God. (Psalm 42:1)"

THE CARS AND THE GARAGE

W
e have a two car garage and for years John would tell me I needed to pull over further. It was a frequent point of contention between us. He'd say, "You need to pull over further, so I have more room." I am not kidding you when I say, I tried.

Finally, one day, I looked at him and said, "If I pull over any further, I'm going to hit the side of the garage!" (Yes, feel free to assume I used a "tone." And it's also safe to assume I considered driving full speed into the garage just to make my point.) "What is it you want me to do?"

John looked at me and, in his calm, logical way, said, "I want you to pull in at an angle, so it allows more room for the car door to open." Moment of silence. Well, why on Earth didn't you say THAT a long time ago? You see, what was perfectly logical inside his brain didn't make any sense in mine. We just think differently. Neither was right, and neither was wrong. We're just different.

Isn't it wonderful that we serve a God Who knows each one of us personally? He not only knows us, but He also created us. He

KISSED BY THE KING

knew exactly what John was saying and exactly what I was saying. (You'd think it wouldn't have taken twenty years to communicate it where we both understood, but I may have actually zoned out for a few years in the middle somewhere.) And He speaks each of our languages. God knows how to speak to me in such a way as I will understand. God knows how to speak to John in a way that he will understand. And God will speak to you in a language you will understand. But we do need to listen. We can't zone out. We can lose a lot of time when we quit paying attention, even if it's because we don't understand. God doesn't mind if we come and ask for clarification. He is always up for a conversation. We could avoid a lot of door dings by listening and following His direction.

As you get into the Word, God will speak. His Holy Spirit is our Counselor. (But the Counselor, the Holy Spirit, whom the Father will send in my name, he will teach you all things, and bring to your remembrance all that I have said to you. [John 14:26]) He knows your learning style, and He will instruct and direct in a way you can understand. Proverbs says, "Trust in the LORD with all your heart and lean not on your own understanding; in all your ways acknowledge Him, and He will direct your paths."

Trust Him. Don't lean on your own understanding. Acknowledge Him. He will direct your paths. The Holy Spirit will teach us all things. He will bring to our remembrance everything God has told us. Just as John and I had to slow down enough to listen to what the other was saying and hear their intention. God is asking us to slow down enough to listen to what He has to say and hear His intention. He loves us!

THE CAR

I've been married to my husband for almost twenty-nine years. One thing has become very clear over our years together. We don't travel well in the same vehicle. It began early on in our married life. I know you all likely have ideal marriages, but we tend to dicker. Why? I'd like to say, "I have no idea." But I strongly suspect it has something to do with two very strong-willed individuals who each want their way. (But seriously, a woman shouldn't need to wear socks in the car during the summer to keep her toes warm!)

We were on a road trip a while back and were having one of those days. I looked at him and said, "You know what? Sometimes you really irritate me." He didn't miss a beat. He replied, "And sometimes you really irritate me."

Pause. I was speechless. Absolutely speechless. I know it's going to seem like an obvious thing to others, but it had never occurred to me that I might irritate him, too. I mean, I suppose if I had dwelt on it for a while, I could have come up with a thing or two I might do that some could find less than perfect. But irritate? Wow.

Of course, I found my voice. I burst out laughing and said, "Really?" He affirmed that he had not misspoken. I'm not sure if it was the raise of his eyebrows or the way his nostrils flared, but according to his body language it was safe to deduct that there are times I bother him. Go figure.

What struck me when thinking back was how easy it is for us to see the faults of others. It often seems certain faults are flashing like a neon sign in the dark. Even though I have struggled with people-pleasing and am usually pretty good at identifying my weaknesses, I don't realize my faults can rub people wrong as well. And if we're honest here, they maybe aren't even faults at all. What is causing the irritation may actually be just a personality trait. Or it could be that I'm struggling with an internal issue that makes me more sensitive to something that would typically not even bother me. How about you? Is there something that can trigger you emotionally and make you a bit more bristly than others? Are there certain people who make your dander go up if you even see them heading your way? Are you aware of your own faults? I'm not for one moment suggesting you begin wallowing in self-condemnation. God clearly speaks to that in the book of Romans. No, I am instead just asking about the scripture in Matthew 6. You know the one. It asks how we can take the speck out of someone else's eye without taking the log out of our own. Regardless of whether you are experiencing irritation or being the irritant, there is a bigger and better point here. What is even more important to remember is that we are forgiven! God doesn't look at you and say, "You are irritating Me." (Although in all fairness, I would deserve it if He did.)

God looks at you and says, "Redeemed. Forgiven. Jesus covered that." As far as the east is from the west, so far He has removed our transgressions from us. And not only that, I suspect it would be one of His heart's greatest desires for us to remember we are loved just the way we are. "But God demonstrates His love for us in this; While we were still sinners, Christ died for us. (Romans 5:8)" He's not waiting for perfection. He's not waiting for you to get it all together before you can come to Him. He's not keeping score or feeling irritated by you. He loves you. He forgives you. He wants a relationship with you. All you need to do is open your arms and your heart and receive it. "Yet to all who did receive him, to those who believed in his name, he gave the right to become children of God. (John 1:12)"

THE SCREWDRIVER

"Be imitators of God, therefore, as beloved children."
Ephesians 5:1

The other day at preschool, we were at recess, and I was watching one of the little guys walk all over the playground with a toy hammer and screwdriver in his hand. Everywhere he went, he was working on the playground equipment. He would bang here, turn there, fixing and adjusting everything he found. I made a comment to the other teacher standing nearby that he even walked like a miniature little man. He was full of confidence, and you could easily see he felt he was able to conquer the world.

An interesting thing happened as he was walking about fixing everything. A couple of girls got their wagon stuck in the pea gravel. Next thing we know, he has stopped fixing the equipment and began to push them out. I said to the other teacher, "Oh, my goodness! Isn't that so nice?!"

Her response, "Yes, (laughing), did you see where he put the screwdriver?" Screwdriver? No. Well, he had stuck it into his pants.

I was in absolute awe. You know what he did, don't you? He was imitating the adults in his life. As they work, they put their tools in their tool belt. I suspect he had watched an adult in his life do carpentry work and put their tools back on their belt when they needed their hands free. And, like any son would do, he imitated his father.

How about you? Are you spending enough time with your Father that you are able to imitate Him? Do you walk like he does? Talk like He does? Share His confidence? Have a joyful spirit? Are you willing to serve like this little boy did? Are you willing to stop what you're doing for a friend in need? I would love nothing more than to wrap that little guy up and give him a hug for being a reflection of what it means to imitate the Father. If you're not sure how our Heavenly Father walks, talks, thinks, acts, I would encourage you to get into the Word and find out. It's all in there. God isn't in the business of hiding Who He is. He wants you to know Him. God yearns for a relationship with you. He wants to be with you, spend time with you, talk to you, hear about your day, and know every up and down you experience. And, as you do, you'll begin to be just like your Dad. You'll be an imitator of God, because you are His beloved child.

Prayer: Father God, please help us to know You. Help us yearn to spend time with You and open Your Word to us so we have understanding and clarity. Be the Light we need as we walk in a dark, dark world. And, Father, please help us know You so deeply that we will imitate you without even realizing it. Because we know You, Dad, and we love You.

Question: What is one thing you can think of today that made you an imitator of Christ

THE EGG

I know nothing about dinosaurs. I have tried to pronounce their names while reading books, and inevitably, I will need to be corrected. I'm okay with it, though. I discovered I can provide wonderful dinosaur activities for children, and they can teach me. This explains how we ended up with these really cool eggs in our sensory table this week. I am going to try and share the three pictures I took. As I looked at them, I was completely amazed at how clearly they showed the sequence God can use in our journey with Him.

The first picture shows the egg whole. It's made out of clay (once you actually read the directions it says "soak them in water first"),

which makes for a bit of a mess right off the bat. The egg comes with this little tool, and the children get to chip away at the eggs trying to discover what is inside. Can you see in the second picture the little foot and a piece of red sticking out at the bottom? Oh, yes, once the chipper begins to see the potential of the dinosaur, they are all in! I rarely see anyone put down the egg once they reach this point. They KNOW there is a dinosaur, and they want it! They are going to work and work until the dinosaur is out. I can't even begin to tell you how diligent the work is! There is rarely even talking between the children working. They just do their thing, knowing if they persist they will find the treasure. And, of course, the last photo shows the dinosaur! It's a bit dirty, because it just came out. It did eventually get washed up. But the joy when the child successfully held it in their hand! Eyes lit up, a huge grin, a true sense of accomplishment.

Do you know we each carry a treasure on the inside of us? Where are you in the process of discovering what yours is? Are you the egg?

Are you at the beginning of your journey with Jesus? Are you willing to surrender to letting Him begin to chip away at your crust? Is He in the process of soaking you so the scraping away of the sin and lies that hold you in bondage can begin? Or are you already undergoing the pain and discomfort that comes with allowing Him access? He isn't out to hurt you. While dying to self can be painful, it's one of the best pains you will ever experience. Because with this pain comes more experienced freedom. There is just so much more if we allow the Holy Spirit access to our heart. Let Him begin the process of bringing down your walls. It may not be a fast process. It may be that Jesus just quietly scrapes away anything that is standing between you and experiencing more of His love and Presence.

One of my favorite pictures was the one where you can see the foot hanging out of the egg. Isn't that hilarious? But it's so symbolic of our heart. As the Savior chips away at your wall, more of who He created you to be will become exposed. The more you embrace and receive His love, the more evident He will become in your life to others. There is a joy that comes with being exposed. You suddenly get to experience love and acceptance in the state of already being known. If we spend life trying to fit in or adapt to how others perceive us, we're missing walking in the fullness of who God created us to be. He has a purpose and a plan for each one of us. However, we need to be willing to be seen. We get to be honest about who we really are. As more of you is revealed in the chipping away process, the more the excitement and joy builds. Why? Because freedom is on the horizon.

Check out that last egg. Well, I guess you can't. The remnants of the egg are still on the dinosaur, but the dinosaur is free. It is no

longer bound by the clay. It can be seen by others. The treasure inside the egg has been revealed. God will continue to wash us as needed. "It is for freedom that Christ has set us free. Stand firm, then, and do not let yourselves be burdened again by a yoke of slavery. (Galatians 5:1)" There is so much awaiting us in our walk with the Savior. A love and grace so deep that we cannot even imagine it. Miracles that unfold in front of our very eyes. Some are big, and everyone gets to see them. Others are private and for our eyes only. We no longer live for the approval of others. We don't need to seek love and acceptance, because we already have it! And as God slowly chips away the wall of lies which can encase us, more and more of His grace, His glory, and His plan will be revealed.

The dinosaur couldn't get itself out of the egg. And we won't get ourselves out of bondage alone. It is in admitting our helplessness and seeking out the Father that we find true freedom. "That is why, for Christ's sake, I delight in weaknesses, in insults, in hardships, in persecutions, in difficulties. For when I am weak, then I am strong." 2 Corinthians 12:10 It is in your very weakness that you are strong. Because Christ is the power and strength inside you! If you can free yourself, others will only see you. As Christ empowers you to walk in more and more of His freedom and love, you become strong. Because it is His strength. His love. His power. His Spirit. His grace. He loves you so very much, He is willing to fill you. Live in you. Empower you. He knows the plans He has for you. "Plans to prosper you and not harm you, plans to give you hope and a future. (Jeremiah 29:11)"

HEY, MRS. WILSON

Have you ever seen the movie, Dennis the Menace? I hope so because it will assist in hearing a voice fluctuation I'm about to share. We were on the second day of the school year when one little guy decided my name was Mrs. Wilson. Randomly, he'd yell out, "Hey, Mrs. Wilson!"

I would chuckle and say, "My name is Mrs. Gustafson."

Five minutes later, "Hey, Mrs. Wilson?"

I'd respond with, "My name is Mrs. Gustafson." This went on all day. I finally stopped telling him my real name and just responded with, "What is my name?" He'd think a moment and eventually began to correct himself. It was my favorite moment of the day. In fact, it's one of my favorites for a long time. There was just something about him yelling my name but not saying it correctly that struck me hilarious!

Aren't you glad Jesus knows your name? In a world where people are busy and rushing from here to there, it can be difficult to feel a deep connection to others. I find myself yearning for a depth that can only develop when I stop long enough to truly know people. "Hi, how are you," as you pass in the grocery store just doesn't quite fill the holes. God created us for relationships. A desire to know and be known. You may only need a community of one, or perhaps you're wired to need a group of 50. Regardless, it's during both the joys and sorrows that we want to be known.

"The gatekeeper opens the gate for him, and the sheep listen to his voice. He calls his own sheep by name and leads them out. (John 10:3)"

If you're feeling alone, there is good news. Jesus knows your name. He won't be yelling, "Hey, Mrs. Wilson" as He speaks to you. He hears your concerns, He shares your joys, and He walks right beside you every single day. Allow Him to come into your presence and receive what He has to offer. Part of walking with Jesus is learning that it's not only about our serving Him. It's also about learning to receive. It's a two-way street. Our service to Jesus will ultimately come out of our love for Him. It won't be a result of obligation, but rather overflow. Let His grace heal your wounds and begin to make room for relationships.

THE FOG

As I left home this morning, the fog was beautiful. I could look across the horizon and see that all the valleys seemed to have fog. It was almost as if God had opened His bag of cotton balls and dumped them into the valleys. The high places were untouched by the denseness, but the bottoms were thick and heavy.

As I drove along, I could see clearly from up on our hill. (I didn't really realize we were on a hill until just now? Go figure.) Yet, I knew those down in the bottoms quite likely didn't have a clear view. They were going to need to wait for the sun to come out and burn away the fog.

Have you ever felt like you're sitting in a fog? Not a great place to be, is it? Maybe you're seeking clarity about something, and the answer just doesn't seem to come. You pray and pray but still the fog feels heavy. Or perhaps God has already given you His answer, and you're just not ready to accept it yet. Still not seeing clearly just yet. What about the pain of loss? The hurt of rejection? The loneliness of a lost friendship?

Or are you the person on the hill today? The view is clear, but you can see your friends and neighbors are being weighed down.

You may not even know their struggles, but you can see the heaviness around them. Perhaps you do know their struggles, but the Son has not yet cleared the fog. You can pray. And pray. And pray.

Whether you are in the fog or on the hill, the answer lies in the same Person. If you're in the fog, hang on! Jesus has promised to never leave you or forsake you. He is in the low place just as He is in the high place. Eventually, the Son will break through that fog and burn it away. You will see Him clearly again. You will again have joy. The difficult season you feel you are in or the pain that seems heavy will be lifted. It may not happen quickly, but it will happen. Jesus said in this world there would be trouble, but we can take heart because He has overcome the world. (John 16:33b)

If you're on the hill, don't be afraid to enter the fog and bring the Spirit of Jesus with you. The Son lives inside you. He's a part of you. As you enter into someone else's fog, you're bringing Jesus. We can be the aroma of Christ. "For we are the aroma of Christ to God among those who are being saved and among those who are perishing, to one a fragrance from death to death, to the other a fragrance from life to life. Who is sufficient for these things? (2 Corinthians 2:15-16)" As you come alongside someone in their valley, you are bringing the hope and joy of Jesus with you. You can be an encourager, supporter, and friend. Be the person who God uses to burn away their loneliness and their fear. Be the person who can lead them to the mountain top (in His timing). "He makes my feet like the feet of a deer; he causes me to stand on the heights. (Proverbs 18:33)"

Whether you're on the mountain or in the valley today, remember Jesus is with you and He has a plan. Our lives have seasons. But whether you are in the fog or on the hill, whether you're in the valley or on the mountain, always keep before you the knowledge of the cross of Jesus. He loves you enough to die for you. He's got you. Trust Him.

THE CANOES AND
THE FLAGS

A s we prepared to make the trip home from MN, we got the notion to bring home our canoes. We've had two stored up in my dad's shed for several years. After discussing it, we determined it might make more sense to sell the canoes and purchase kayaks instead. The canoes are very heavy, and dad had one suspended from the ceiling. It was always just a challenge to use them, and we thought the kayaks might be easier.

And, blessings abound. My younger brother decided he'd like to buy both canoes. He and his family like to float the river, and the canoes will work out perfect for them. He said he would get them next year with his trailer. But my hubby is rather creative and decided since we had two vehicles, perhaps we could haul them in the back of the pickup.

I invite you to try and picture the scene ahead of our car on the drive home. John is in the pickup in front of us with the canoes. I must say, he did a fantastic job of securing them. We didn't see them bouncing around at all. Most of you probably know that if you're going to haul something like this (aka more canoe out of the pickup than in), you are required to tie a flag on the back. It allows people in other vehicles to gauge the depth perception and not run into the back end. Those "flags" were whipping around, and every so often a chunk would land on our vehicle. However, they served their purpose, and the canoes are now safely in Iowa.

As I watched the towel waving around (we didn't actually have flags, so we improvised), it reminded me of the way hurting people act. As much as we all crave relationships and are designed for them, people who have been hurt can struggle with receiving love. You've probably heard the saying that "hurting people hurt people." If you get too close, it's almost as if they're waving a flag. It's warning you to get back. What does their flag look like? Well, quite likely they're not waving a towel. Perhaps they are bitey in their tone. Have you met anyone who is super friendly but isn't comfortable opening up? What about the person you know who is bitter? Rude? Vindictive? Just difficult? As you begin to establish a relationship with someone carrying unhealed hurts, don't be surprised if they begin to wave a flag.

God didn't call us to just love those easy to love. He said to love our enemies. Bless them. Pray for them. The harder their flag waves, the more we can rejoice because the Holy Spirit is working. Don't give up! The same God who began a good work in you and will carry it on to completion until the day of Christ Jesus has begun one in them too. (Philipians 1:6) You can be part of their healing. You may get hit with a flying chunk of towel in the process, but don't be deterred. Perfect love can cast out their fear of being hurt again. (1 John 4:18) It's not you loving them. It's God in you. It's the gift of Jesus which you received free of charge paid at His expense. You can share the gift. He is more than plenty to go around. I can't wait to hear who God puts in your path to love on this week. Remember, the flags waving may be saying "Be careful, I'm hurting." But the healing love of Jesus through you can assist someone in arriving at their destination in Jesus.

LET'S GO CANOEING

T oday we were out canoeing. My daughter was in the front and I in the back. It took us a while to find our rhythm, but gliding across the water made it all worthwhile. If you've ever been in a canoe, you know that both people need to work together. And they both will need to anticipate which direction they want the canoe to go. The person in the back does most of the steering, but the person in front can make that job much easier by paddling on the same side of the canoe to get it to turn faster. It takes a lot longer and is much less efficient if you're not working together.

Our destination was the far side of the lake where all the lily pads were. They were just starting to bloom a beautiful yellow flower. The water was rather shallow there, so a fishing boat couldn't make it back that far, but the canoe just glided over the water. It allowed us to investigate all sorts of fun places which we'd otherwise miss.

What lessons did God teach me on this venture? First, He is the One in the back of our life canoe. He will steer and direct where He wants us to go. However, if we listen and work with Him and go where He tells us, we'll get there much easier and smoother. And when the big winds come, if we cooperate and trust Him, we'll make it through together.

Second, the lily pad destination taught me that when God's in the boat, the destination is always much more beautiful than if we were in the boat alone. If I had tried to maneuver my way to that section of the lake independently, I never would have made it. Someone with more experience may have, but I know I wouldn't have. I was exhausted as it was. If we allow God to drive our boat and trust His lead, He will show us beauty we never would have seen otherwise. Ephesians 3:20 says "He is able to do immeasurably more than we could ask, think or even imagine." Just chew on that awhile! You can't even imagine the places He wants to take you and show you. It's better than our brains would even be able to conjure up on our own. Surrender and enjoy!

PLEASE, WEAR YOUR LIFE JACKET

We have been on the river kayaking the past couple of days. Yesterday was our first time down the Boyer, so we weren't really certain what to expect. We would hit an occasional small rapid, which would add just a touch of excitement. As we were coming around one bend, my daughter commented that she could hear something. As we got closer, we could see rapids that were going to be a little bit rougher. As fast as I could, I started paddling back upstream. I had put my life jacket on when we heard the rapids, but I didn't have it zipped. I decided by the looks of things, I needed it zipped. (My very wise daughter was already all zipped into hers when I turned around.)

Today as we were heading down the river again, and we got to the same spot, my daughter was telling the story to our guest about how I hightailed it out of there yesterday. Apparently, she felt I had deserted her at a very important moment. I had no argument, because I did. My motivation wasn't avoidance at the cost of my daughter going first, but instead, self-protection. I could see danger and needed to get zipped into the life jacket.

Who and what are your "life jackets" when you hit the rapids of life? Sometimes life is floating along all peaceful and smooth, and you're just being carried by the current of the day. You may have a forewarning that trouble could be coming. Maybe you'll hear it like we heard the rapids around the bend. Perhaps you round the bend and see it. Trouble. What is your reaction going to be when you see it coming? What can you do to be prepared in advance?

What set of rapids has life thrown your way? Job loss? Someone you love is sick? Your health has hit a roadblock? Lots of unexpected financial expenses? Perhaps there are uncontrollable issues with your children, parents, or close friends? Perhaps something others can't see? Depression? Anxiety? Loneliness? Maybe you had time and were forewarned that trouble was coming. But maybe you rounded the bend, and there it was. A curve ball is thrown at you by life. What now?

God tells us very clearly in Ephesians 6:11-18 to put on the full armor of God. **"Put on the whole armor of God, that you may be able to stand against the schemes of the devil. For we do not wrestle against flesh and blood, but against the rulers, against the authorities, against the cosmic powers over this present darkness, against the spiritual forces of evil in the heavenly places. Therefore, take up the whole armor of God, that you may be able to withstand in the evil day,**

SEE IT, BE IT

The other day, I was standing in the bathroom looking in the mirror. I happened to notice the reflection of the beautiful redbud tree outside our window. It is absolutely gorgeous right now. The delicate pink flowers are adding a striking color to our backyard which is quietly waking up from its winter rest. I stood for a moment and just admired the color before I turned around and looked out the window. The reflection was beautiful and worth the time to see, but it didn't compare to the real deal. The reflection caught sight of the top of the tree. However, a look out the window revealed a gnarled tree trunk which showed age and character. The low branches could use a trimming to ease mowing, but their access to reach out and touch made the tree approachable and able to engage with. Yes, the reflection caught my eye, but the reflection was only a glimpse of the real beauty of the tree.

I first thought this message from the Lord was going to be the importance of seeing the beauty right in front of us. We often go about our day and don't stop to see the beautiful blessings God has placed in our lives. They are there to be enjoyed, but sometimes they are positioned so we need to turn around to truly appreciate them. However, I realized there was a bigger lesson for me. I loved the gift of the tree in the mirror. I mean, really, who gets to enjoy the beauty of the outdoors in their bathroom? Yet that glimpse of creation was nothing compared to taking the time to turn around and absorb the entirety of the beauty the whole tree presented.

Can you see it? It is who **we** are **in Christ**. It is what we're called to be. We're a reflection of the One Who created us. Do people see you and catch a reflection of Jesus? Do you come into their world and leave a desire for them to want to see God Himself? Oh, we will never be God, but God does in fact live in us. "Do you not know that your body is a temple of the Holy Spirit, who is in you, whom you have received from God? You are not your own; you were bought at a price," says 1 Corinthians 6:19. But the more we rest in His love and spend time in His presence, He will change our lives. He is so much more. I have no idea why it can be such a battle to surrender at times. His way is never wrong and always, always for our best. The more we let go of what we think will fill and make us happy and choose His way, the more joy and peace we will walk in. The more we will reflect the Creator and His Son. I pray our lives will be a reflection of the love of the Father. I pray others will see just a glimpse of Him in us. I pray the world can know Jesus in all His glory and love!

"Greater love has no one than this: to lay down one's life for one's friends. You are my friends if you do what I command. I no longer call you servants, because a servant does not know his master's business. Instead, I have called you friends, for everything that I learned from my Father I have made known to you. You did not choose me, but I chose you and appointed you so that you might go and bear fruit—fruit that will last—and so that whatever you ask in my name the Father will give you. (John 15:13-16)"

TRUSTING HIM

Friday afternoons are my errand days. Do you ever have those? All those places you need to stop just for a quick little something. I usually begin by enjoying it and end up utterly exhausted, tired of people, and just wanting to go home and sit down. One of the fun things to do is listen to speakers while I'm driving in the car to pass the time. I was about mid-way through a favorite sermon when I arrived in a nearby town. Once those errands were completed, I appreciated the thirty-minute return drive, which allowed me to finish the sermon. There was a very simple take away for me on that day. He stated that salvation is dependent upon grace not works, but a victorious, joy-filled, Christian life is rooted in obedience. (He said it much better than I did. I am paraphrasing here.)

Obedience. There was a time when hearing the word obedience made me cringe. It felt like work the church was trying to pile on its members. Those expectations required to be accepted. But the longer I have walked with the Lord, I realize how skewed my perception of obedience was. Obedience is just walking out our faith. It's knowing we are loved unconditionally by Someone Who only wants our best. It's doing what God asks out of trust and dependence. It's taking hold of my Father's hand and walking together through life.

Okay, back to the errands. I had just finished my last stop at the local Walmart. And it was a big one this time. The cart was full. I got everything rung up and wheeled the cart out to the parking lot to unload. As I was in the process, one of our daughters called and asked if I could pick something up for her. "No, I'm already out of the store and in the parking lot." Admit it; you would not have wanted to go back in either. While we're talking, I'm thinking to myself, "Be strong and just say no." It was during this internal conversation with myself that I noticed a little box of ornament hooks in the bottom of the cart. I remembered seeing the price when I picked them up. They cost 98 cents. And I knew I had forgotten to ring them up, because they had been hidden under another box! No. No. No.

This is when the Holy Spirit pulls up the Word He'd just placed in my heart. Obedience is trusting God's way is the best. I had not paid for the 98 cent ornament hooks, and the honest thing to do was go back into the store. (Did I mention I was parked in Row 6? You know the one waaaay on the other side of the parking lot from the door.) I finished storing everything away, grabbed the 98 cent hooks, pulled the mask back out of my pocket (because let's face it, wearing the mask is not a motivator to return to the store), and I headed back inside. I paid for the hooks (bonus for the daughter because now I could pick up what she wanted also) and headed back to the car. Honestly, I was now a little less exhausted, too. Why? Because living a life of obedience brings joy. And while it seemed a small thing, it was an obedience issue. Was I going to be honest? Was I going to demonstrate integrity? Was I going to trust my Dad?

Luke 5 tells of the time Jesus hopped in a boat and taught the crowds from the water. Once He was finished, he told Simon Peter to go out deeper and throw out the nets. Peter's response to Jesus was (paraphrased), "We fished all night and have little to show for it. (Aka we're exhausted). But because You are telling us to do it, we will." Obedience. He didn't do it out of fear of judgment or punishment. Peter obeyed because he TRUSTED the heart of Jesus. He'd hung out with Him enough to know Jesus was FOR him. By the way, they caught so many fish the nets started to break, and they called for another boat to come. It took two boats to get the catch back to shore, and both were almost sinking from all the fish. God blessed Peter's obedience. God will bless your obedience.

What is God asking you to do today? Where can you demonstrate your love to Him by stepping out in faith and obedience? It might be as simple as returning and paying for the hooks. It might be spending extra time in prayer. Perhaps He has been asking you to check in on a friend. Or maybe it's more time in the Word (which FYI will be the compass to know how to obey). Regardless of what He is asking you to do, I want to encourage you to trust Him. After all, He gave His Son to die in our place so we can spend eternity with Him. I'd say He's earned it!

BUTTERFLIES

One day I was out driving and noticed there were hundreds of millions of butterflies! (This is NOT an exaggeration!) They were everywhere! I was driving to town and called John to ask if he had also noticed them. Yep. I said, "Hon, I can't miss them! They're everywhere, and I don't like killing all these butterflies." You know, because butterflies are delicate and beautiful.

His response shocked me, "Hit as many as you can and kill them!" What on earth? He said, "They're the bad kind eating our crops."

Hmmm, I still didn't go out of my way to kill butterflies. But death was unavoidable because they were absolutely everywhere. I thought the lesson they taught was a valuable one. What I had perceived as a beautiful, delicate part of God's creation was, in fact, deadly to the bean crop. It's why the helicopters and airplanes had been buzzing all the fields of late.

As believers, we need to pray to be constantly discerning. Matthew 7:15 tells us "Beware of false prophets, which come to you in sheep's clothing, but inwardly they are ravening wolves." Not everything and everyone that looks like a good thing is a good thing.

"I am sending you out like sheep among wolves. Therefore, be as shrewd as snakes and as innocent as doves. (Matthew 10:16)" You see, just like the butterflies which appeared beautiful, they were actually sucking the life right out of the plants.

If you find someone who appears to be "all that" on the outside, be sure to check where their heart is. Be kind. Be polite. Share the Gospel. But be cautious and aware. You don't want to be led into deception by outward appearance. Appearances can be deceiving. We want to be led by the Spirit of the Living God. We want Jesus to be at the heart and center of all of our decisions and actions.

And, on a side note, not everything that looks bad really is. Remember Joseph, he was sold into slavery by his brothers. (Genesis 37) Not good, right? He was obedient and rose into a position of importance only to be mistreated by lies and thrown into prison. Again, not great circumstances. BUT, what looked bad was really being used as part of God's plan to save the land of Israel during a drought. Didn't get the job you'd hoped for? Maybe God is protecting your family instead. Were you hoping for that new house, and the deal fell through? Perhaps you're being protected from something. Our job is to trust the Redeemer. Jesus always, always, always has your back. He is completely for you. He loves you like crazy. Be cautious not to make your judgement by the outward appearance. What is sometimes beautiful can be deadly for your spiritual harvest. What appears awful and brings disappointment can actually be God's hand of love, because He has a better plan.

The bottom line, "Surely God is my salvation; I will trust and not be afraid. The LORD, the LORD himself, is my strength and my defense; He has become my salvation. (Isaiah 12:2)" Stop judging by mere appearances, but instead judge correctly. (John 7:24)"

CHOSEN

A couple weeks ago while attending our town's summer festivities, we went to check out a batch of puppies someone had brought along for sale. You know the Scripture that says, "There hath no temptation taken you, but such is common to man…? (1 Corinthians 10:15a)" Well, we didn't resist the temptation. We came home with a new puppy! And it is quite interesting how it all transpired. We went to look at where the puppies were all running around, and I began lobbying. Both John and I knew our dog was getting older and had been keeping our eyes out for a new pup. Once we saw the little pups, I was hooked.

As I was cuddling one of the pups and doing a bit of adult begging, John just kept saying "no, no, no." (Two weeks in and dog allergies that make breathing difficult, I'm thinking, once again, I should have listened to him.) We were walking away from the puppies empty handed when John said, "If we were going to get one, I'd want the one that was laying on the ground." Whoa! Did he just open the door for a pup? We turned around and headed back to see which one he had spotted.

There she was, just laying there on the ground. She wasn't up and zipping around like the other pups, but just lounging. She was adorable. She appeared more of a red heeler than blue. I said, "If you want that one, I'm good with it." And that was it. We now have this adorable little puppy who no longer just lays around. She has completely taken over the hearts of the entire family. She's smart. She's cute. She's funny. Even Freckles has finally decided not to chew her up in one big bite. Even more interesting (but not surprising), John seems to be the favorite between the two of us. If he's not around (and she's in the house, which we're trying to break this bad habit), she will run, stand by his chair, and whimper. She will even lay at the foot of the chair waiting for his return.

I share all these details because it reminds me a lot of our walk with Jesus. Did you catch how Kentucky (our puppy's name) came to live with us? John **chose** him. I had another pup in my hands, but John knew which one would be a good fit for our family. God has done the same thing. He chose us. "...just as He chose us in Him before the foundation of the world, that we would be holy and blameless before Him in love... (Ephesians 1:4)" Wow! The verse says he chose us before the foundation of the world. It means we were created with purpose. He chose us before He even formed us in our mother's wombs! And He did it in love.

Sometimes we may pick up messages whether true or not that we are not wanted. We are not loved. We are not important. But those messages are false. Are you going to believe what the world says about you or remember that you are here on this earth because God chose you! Hey, Someone loves me enough to choose me and design me with a purpose. I'm going to go hang out at the foot of His chair just as Kentucky does to John. I'll spend time there. Rest in the knowledge that in this place I am special, and I am loved.

Side note: Guess what the result can be? We've been super concerned about Kentucky with our big dog, Freckles. Freckles can be a bit aggressive, especially when feeling jealous or protective. Well, yesterday, I watched as Kentucky actually chased Freckles all

KISSED BY THE KING

over the yard. She had no fear. The more you hang out at the foot of the Master, your fear will also dissipate. Just because someone you know (or don't know) has a bit of a bite or a loud bark, doesn't mean you need to fear them. You'll have the power of Jesus to engage in play or even chase them off if necessary. The power of the Love of Jesus!

THE BRIDGE

We had a return trip to the oral surgeon today. After we left his office, we headed to Target to make an exchange. We were driving over one of those overpass bridges with walls not quite high enough for my taste. I have this little "fear of heights" thing going on and being up there did nothing to soothe my anxiety. I mean, honestly, if God wanted us way up there, it seems like He would have given us wings so we could fly. I commented that I wished the sides were higher so I wouldn't even need to see over the edge. Abbie said, "I love the view from up here. It's beautiful!"

Uh, ya, right. It jarred loose a memory of a track coach who told me that if you keep your eyes on the back of the runner in front of you, you'll just pull yourself into them. You don't want to look back, because you'll lose your momentum. Just fix your eyes on the target where you're going until you get there. Personally, I thought it was very applicable advice on the bridge. I had no intention of looking over the edge and enjoying the view. (Maybe I should mention Abbie was driving so keeping my eyes closed was a legitimate option.) But, if I kept my eyes on the road in front of me or one of the cars ahead, I could just pull myself into the road and soon found myself at the bottom of the bridge.

I'm sure in an attempt to ease my jittery nerves, Abbie tells me that it really takes a lot of trust to believe those bridges will even hold us up. She's, like, "Look, Mom. Look how long it is. This thing could be lined with cars, and everyone just believes the bridge will hold them up." Yep. Super, duper helpful.

Can you see the connection between the three? Following Jesus requires that same kind of faith and trust. We just know He's going to hold us up. He's way more dependable than concrete. The Bible says, "Now faith is confidence in what we hope for and assurance about what we do not see. (Hebrews 11:1)" We can't see Jesus in the physical sense, but we know beyond a shadow of a doubt He's with us. We are confident He is at work in our lives all of the time. Oh, trusting isn't always easy. Personally, I've had something nagging at the back of my mind today. I can feel it's going to turn into full-blown fretting if I don't go get my Bible and hang out with Jesus tonight. But I know that as soon as I enter into the presence of our King and spend time in His Word, my attitude will change. Because Scripture says "...faith comes from hearing and hearing from the Word of God. (Romans 10:17)"

You know how Abbie was enjoying the view, and I was zeroed in on the road ahead? I'm not sure either is right or wrong. God tells us to "Fix our eyes on Jesus, the Author and Perfecter of our faith. (Hebrews 12:2)" I had my eyes fixed. I was focusing on what was getting me through the stressful situation. (Keep in mind, I'm embellishing the fear a bit.) But it is how I handle heights while driving. I absolutely can't look around. I have to keep my eyes focused on the road ahead. Just as Christ is asking me to fix my eyes upon Him. He wrote my faith and will perfect it. Oh, my faith isn't done and neither is yours. We'll keep growing until the day we meet Jesus in our new home above. Romans 12:3 says, "For by the grace given to me I say to everyone among you not to think of himself more highly than he ought to think, but to think with sober assigned." I've wondered what a measure of faith is before, and I've asked God to give me a double portion if that is allowed. One thing I know for certain, I want all the faith He is willing to give. It's a gift. It's nothing we can get on our own. It's given to us by His amazing and unexplainable grace.

I want to end with the view. There I was focused on the road. (Good plan, it got me where I needed to be.) But all the while I was looking straight ahead, Abbie's chatting away enjoying the view. You've likely heard the verse, "...but those who hope in the LORD will renew their strength. They will soar on wings like eagles; they will run and not grow weary, they will walk and not be faint." She chose to soar at that moment. Not only did she arrive at her destination, but she enjoyed the beauty along the way. God's not in the business of getting angry at our approach to demonstrate faith. He is about loving us. Growing us. Meeting us where we're at. "Faith the size of a mustard seed can move a mountain. "...you can say to this mountain, 'Move from here to there,' and it will move. Nothing will be impossible for you. (Matthew 17:20b)" So you see, trusting and having faith may look different at different times in your life. Sometimes you'll zero in, fix your eyes on Jesus, and literally let His love pull you in and lead you through. Other times, you will trust Him so much you'll soar. You'll believe, relax, and enjoy the view. I suspect Abbie's way was more rewarding for her, but who knows? Given time, I might be sneaking a peak or soaring with the eagles myself.

A BIGGER LOAD

W e took a road trip this morning to Council Bluffs. (No one in our home any longer possesses wisdom teeth.) On the way home, I was shocked at the amount of traffic on the interstate. I've driven it many times and have never seen that many cars. It's kind of interesting to watch people as they drive. You have those who are slow and steady in the right lane, those who zip back and forth convinced they'll achieve their final destination that much sooner, and then those who want to fly down the road and hope no one has on their radar gun. I had to chuckle today suspecting that the fast lane wasn't moving quite as rapidly as some would have wanted. There were times the cars seemed to be five or six deep with the lead car in the fast lane going just a touch faster than the slow lane. (I know, maddening if you're the one at the back of the pack.)

If you've ever turned off an interstate and shifted to the 55-mph speed limit, you know the level of self-control required after driving 70. Ugh. We found ourselves, again, behind a semi. As I was calmly and patiently enjoying my drive behind said semi, I began to experience this overwhelming empathy for the semi drivers. It seems that no matter what they do, someone is always passing them. They have no choice but to adapt to speed going up hills, which results in them often not getting to lead the pack. And after watching yet another semi come down the road and have a car go whizzing past, it seemed to hit me plain as day. "Of course, they're going slower, have you seen the size of their load?"

Ouch. I felt the Spirit sort of tap me on the shoulder. "Did you catch that one, Leslie?"

"Yes, I heard it and I'm thinking it may have pinched a bit as You tapped me!" You see, as we go about life, we (okay, I, but it would sure feel better if I wasn't alone) can find ourselves sometimes being judgmental about things we know absolutely nothing about. You know, the people who have struggles that look different than our own? There are certain situations which are just frustrating and push our buttons. We find ourselves wrapped up in a ball of tense just because people aren't doing things the way we would do them. But we really do need to pause and remember, they may be carrying a much larger load than we are.

The semi driver was heading where he needed to be going. But the load he was required to carry was very different from the load in my car. God doesn't ask the same of everyone. Our relationships with Him are personal. I may be asked to do just one or two things today versus another who has been asked to do many. We really don't know what other people are dealing with. Even those whom we see every day. There are things they can't talk about. Pain that seems so deep they feel they may break to share it. But, maybe, just maybe, you're the person called to help them carry their load. Or perhaps you're the person God has called to walk beside them as they carry it. (When Moses' hands grew tired, they took a stone and put it under him, and he sat on it. Aaron and Hur held his hands up—one on one side, one on the other—so that his hands remained steady till sunset. [Exodus 17:12]) Or maybe your role is prayer. (And pray in the Spirit on all occasions with all kinds of prayers and requests. With this in mind, be alert and always keep on praying for all the Lord's people. [Ephesians 6:18]) The important thing is whether we're driving the semi or zipping along in a sports car, we can be compassionate. We can show the love of Christ. We can be His hands and feet. (There was not a needy person among them, for as many as were owners of lands or houses sold them and brought the proceeds of what was sold and laid it at the apostles' feet, and it was distributed to each as any had need. [Acts 4:34-35])

"Come to me, all you who are weary and burdened, and I will give you rest. Take my yoke upon you and learn from me, for I am gentle and humble in heart, and you will find rest for your souls. For my yoke is easy and my burden is light. (Matthew 11:28-30)"

PERFECT LOVE
CASTS OUT FEAR

C an you still remember the games and activities you participated in as a child? I grew up on a farm, and looking back, life seemed so simple. I don't think there was hardly a speck of soil our feet didn't touch at one point or another. The rock pile at the end of the lane, the little trail that led behind the machine shed, or even the tree we'd grab hold of as we would swing off the playhouse. (I can hardly believe my mother allowed us to swing off the roof of the playhouse, but I suspect she must not have known.) I can remember the challenge presented one day to sit in the hay mound and attempt to jump to the ground. It certainly seemed a long way down at the time, but eventually the leap was made successfully without injury. Does reflection into your childhood entertainment bring a smile to your face? Or are your memories a source of pain? I do hope there was joy to be latched onto.

My dad had a corn crib, and every once in a while we'd crawl up the ladder to see what was up there. I don't remember going up there very often, and the thought of two ladders sticks in my mind. It seems we had to crawl up one, turn, and continue to crawl up another. (I may need to go check out whether the memory is accurate next time I'm home on the farm.) If I recall, there were rules that we weren't supposed to be up there because of the grain in the bins. Regardless, I know at one time or another, I must have managed to get up there since I seem to have snippets of recollection. How did I even do that without being terrified? I may have been motivated by a need to keep up with my brothers? Regardless, the years have resulted in muscles which aren't quite as agile and an increased "awareness" of heights. So, it was no surprise when going with John to work on tearing shiplap off the walls in an old corn crib this week, I was not super excited about making the journey up the ladder. John just kept saying, "Don't look down." I listened, and up I went.

The old saying, "What goes up must come down" was rolling around in my head as I tried to play out how exactly "down" was going to be managed. It took me a good half an hour to relax just wondering about how I'd get back out of there. John went down for a drink midway, but I opted to stay put because the entire process of trying to get out was overwhelming. Why? Because I was afraid!

Well, as you can guess, I couldn't move in a mattress and sleep with the raccoon poop so at some point I was going to HAVE to climb down. Let me just say, my husband was a prince. He first situated himself in the opening by the ladder to offer support. (Great! Now we'd both fall!) He then removed all the boards around the ladder to allow for me to remain standing and simply step onto the ladder without squatting down. He provided all sorts of coaching on not looking down and kept encouraging me that I would be fine. But I just have to tell you, fear is a real thing. I KNEW it was no big deal. I KNEW I could fall out of there and live. I KNEW I would be fine. However, the space between my head and my heart seemed quite a distance when it came to trusting my husband.

There were so many lessons in that moment. First of all, there are times we are going to have to take the leap of faith and climb the ladder not knowing how we'll get back down. Scripture says, "Thy Word is a lamp unto my feet and a light unto my path. (Psalm 119:105)" Sometimes when you're walking in the dark with a flashlight, you only get to see the five feet in front of you. You don't get to see the destination. What is God asking you to do today that you want to know the end of the story? Is He asking you to step out in faith and obey? You can deal with the details as they come. The fear you may be feeling to obey Him in a new way "feels" real. Let's face it, fear is a real emotion. What are you going to do with it? I started praying the moment I got up in the corn crib about how I was going to get down. I finally parked the fear and just helped with removing boards. However, I was praying full on when it was time to go down that ladder. Don't forget, "Perfect Love casts out fear." As we step into the presence of God, He will remove the fear bit by bit.

Remember how John was such an example of who Jesus is? I pray I will never forget that moment. He wedged himself into that space to assure me I would not fall. No, I didn't trust Him, but it does not change the fact he was there. It's the same way with God. He promises us in His Word that "...He will never leave us or forsake us. (Deuteronomy 31:8)" He is right there ready to catch us. Honestly, I can hardly believe my husband didn't yell at me. I would have lost my patience or left and gone home. Nope. He began removing the shiplap around the hole to make the descent easier. I pointed out that now there was nothing protecting a person from tripping and falling out unexpectedly. How often does God provide a way, and we turn it around? God is always going to make a way. He LOVES us. He won't leave us in fear. But at some point, we need to take that first step of faith. We have to step into the fear to experience God's faithfulness.

Obviously, I got down from the corn crib. I prayed. I prayed. I prayed some more. John never said a word. He did make the observation that the praying took a while before it seemed to take effect in my mind. He was right. The Truth was just taking time to trickle down to my heart. Do you want to know what's really cool? Once I got down, I was able to go up and down several times without fear. I ran down to grab a tool. I crawled back up carrying a big pry bar. Once you trust God "in the fear," you will find that you are able to do it again and again. And each time you repeat it, God may give you more responsibility.

What is God asking you to step into today? He won't give up on you so don't feel like you're too afraid to be helped. God doesn't work that way. It may be baby steps for you, or it may be a giant leap. Regardless, He will be balanced to catch you. He will remove the boards to make the same hole look safer. He will encourage. He will go with you. As I became more at ease ascending and descending to the upstairs of the corn crib, I began paying attention to the ladder. Do you want to know what I found amazing? The boards of the ladder were actually worn from years of other people putting their hands and feet on them. The Bible is full of examples of people who have stepped into fear and trusted God's leading. His Spirit is here to empower us to obey. I'd encourage you to ask yourself today if there is anything God is asking you to do that you've been holding off on because of fear. (FYI: Fear likes to disguise itself as a tricky word from time to time. AKA, "Concern," "I don't want to offend anyone," "What if," etc.) Begin praying and ask God how He wants you to step into the fear and begin watching for His provision. We have His Spirit living inside us. We are His children. We are not slaves to fear. God has given us authority over the darkness, and His perfect love will send fear a- packing. We are victors. You are a victor. Go ahead, you may be the first one to imprint the ladder for generations coming behind you. Trust Him. He's worth it!

BUT I CAN'T SEE

Have you ever been around someone who viewed life from a completely different perspective than you? Better yet, have you ever been asked to work on a project or committee with that type of person? Ultimately, you would both get the work completed, but your approach looks nothing alike. How does it make you feel? Does it feel like a great challenge, and you engage in discovering how that person sees the world? Or, let's be honest here, does it drive you just a little bit batty? Do you want to drop everything, put your hands on your hips, give a little glare, and say, "Really, your way makes absolutely NO SENSE whatsoever to a 'logical' person?" Maybe, just maybe, you're even married to this person. Smile.

This weekend, we had the pleasure of helping our daughter move into her new home. Can you just envision it? The temperature was over 90 degrees, the furniture was bulky and heavy, and guess what, our approach was very different when it came to carrying the larger items. We would pull something out of the back end of the pickup, and we would prepare for the walk across the lawn. Abbie liked to go backward or forward depending on which side she was standing. I, however, wanted to carry the item between us and walk straight ahead. You know, so we could walk side by side. I'd get a hold of my end and immediately begin to turn us. Abbie had finally had enough and said, "Mom, why do you keep trying to turn us?" I responded with my typical burst of laughter (this happens when something strikes me funny and one of my children is exasperated with me) and said, "I like to see where I'm going!" (Exclamation point included because remember it was 90 plus degrees, and after the burst of laughter, I may or may not have been feeling a bit irritable.)

Wow! I was immediately struck by how often this is my response to God. He is in the lead (although I don't picture Him actually walking backwards), and it feels like there is a giant sofa between us, and I am unable to see. He is leading and asking me to just follow. I don't need to see where I'm going, because I'm not in charge of the destination. BUT I really want to turn us so I can see where we're going. Or maybe I'm even thinking His approach makes no logical sense, and we should do it differently. Have you wanted to see where God is taking you rather than just following in obedience? Or, have you wanted to approach the situation your own way? Do you have a loved one that is struggling with something? Do you wish you could fix it for them? Or perhaps it doesn't need to be fixed; you just have to surrender that it isn't being done your way. (Ouch, I felt that one! I REALLY like to have things done my way!) Are you wanting to tackle a project at home or work, but you don't feel your voice is being heard? Are you watching someone walk out a life filled with joy, and their approach makes no sense? (It doesn't always have to be a problem that is approached differently. Sometimes, it can just be life in general.) You'd like to experience the same level of joy they are, but their approach just doesn't make sense to you. Regardless of whether you are experiencing frustration because a problem isn't being dealt with as you think it should or whether you're desiring a joy you don't have, the answer can be the same. I'd encourage you to grab your Bible and check out Psalm 119:105, "Thy word is a lamp unto my feet, and a light unto my path."

A life walked with Jesus is the only true source of joy we will ever know. Do you want to be the person walking around filled with joy (even when you're struggling)? You can have it! You just need to surrender and allow Jesus to direct how and where you're walking. Are you wanting to walk side by side so you can see where you're going? Yes, I prefer that approach myself. But when God told Abraham to pack up his belongings and get ready to move (Genesis 12:1), He didn't tell him where he was going. Abraham knew that God could be trusted, because He loved him. He also knew that sometimes the lamp lighting up his path only showed him the next step. (Think about it in terms of a flashlight in this situation. A flashlight only lights up enough of the path so you can see where you go next, it doesn't illuminate the entire highway all the way to the neighboring town.) Therefore, Abraham packed up for the move! The longer we walk with God, the more we know His heart is for us. He loved us enough to send His one and only Son to die in our place. (John 3:16) If He did that for us, I'm pretty sure whatever He asks us to do is for our best. And since He is for our best, His approach to life is for our best as well. It is worth doing it His way. He will never lead us where He won't keep us (we can park our fears and desire to be in control of the outcome). "Since you are my rock and my fortress, for the sake of your name lead and guide me. (Psalm 31:3)"

There is a difference between allowing Jesus to be your Savior and allowing Him to be your Lord. Do you trust that God loves you so much He sent His Son to die in your place? Accepting this Truth makes Jesus your Savior. If you desire to walk the day to day with Jesus doing life "His Way," requires you to allow Him to be Lord of your life. You will get to listen to Him speak, follow His lead, laugh with Him, cry with Him, talk to Him, get angry and vent with Him (really, I can't be the only one), and sometimes just sit beside Him and enjoy being together. He will ask you to trust Him. Remember that first verse? His Word is a lamp unto your feet and a light to your path? As you get into the Word, you will see what His will is and His desire for your life. It will be the most fun-filled and joy-filled journey! It may also be terrifying at times, because He will want to stretch you. (It's why He says "fear not" so many times in Scripture.) Today is the day to surrender just a little bit more (or a lot more). If you haven't done it yet, today is a great day to make Him your Savior. Ask Him to forgive you for your sins and invite Him to come and live inside your heart. He is waiting and ready! Already know Jesus? Today is a great day to trust Him as Lord of your life. Quit trying to see where you're going. Stop trying to dictate what road He takes you on. Let others approach their walk with Jesus the way He's asking them to go, and you follow where He's directing you. He is asking you to "Enter through the narrow gate. For wide is the gate and broad is the road that leads to destruction, and many enter through it. But small is the gate and narrow the road that leads to life, and only a few find it. (Matthew 7:13-14)"

Come on, let's go! Today is the day of full surrender. He's only asking you to take one step at a time. You don't have to run, just walk. Jesus has got you right in the palm of His hand. Trust Him to lead you in the best direction for your life. Grab your Bible and go see what the next step for you looks like.

Then Jesus told him, "Because you have seen me, you have believed; blessed are those who have not seen and yet have believed. (John 20:29)"

THE BUNKS

We had a machine shed just south of our house. I used to ask John if we could move it so I could see the pond. You can all but guess what the answer was. No. Apparently, you don't move large buildings just to give your wife a view of the pond. I told him I was going to pray and ask God to move the machine shed for me. Yes, God is so very good. He DID move that machine shed for us! A couple of years ago during a storm, the wind picked the machine shed up, snapped the foundational posts, and set it right back down. It turned out the wood was unsafe, and the shed would need to officially come down. Please keep in mind, I'm not advocating that you pray to God and ask Him to remove your buildings when there is nothing wrong with them and you just have a whimsical notion to see the landscape. But I won't deny that when the decision was made the building couldn't be salvaged and would need to be removed, I was more than a little convinced it was God's doing. He had a better plan.

It has been great fun watching His plan unfold, too. John acquired a handful of cattle bunks, and we decided to use a portion of the big cement slab to set up a little area for raised-bed gardening. It's been quite a process. The bottoms of the bunks were covered with rock (this is to allow the water to pass through), and the top was covered in soil. We worked diligently the other night to get a couple of the bunks ready before it rained. As John continued to haul the dirt, I decided to stick the tomato plants in one of the bunks. The day had been long, the dirt was clumpy, and I was tired. I guesstimated where the plants should go and stuck them in the soil. After getting everything put away, I headed to the house to collapse into a chair. (Yes, I'm being a bit overly dramatic, but it was 8:30 p.m. by this point, and I had worked all day.) Well, John parked his tractor, and as I waited, he didn't come into the house. It was starting to get dark enough I thought I should maybe go check on him when he came inside. I asked what he was doing, and he told me he'd been planting his strawberry plants. It didn't seem like it should have taken that long until he explained his process. He had been first preparing his soil before he planted his strawberries.

It was not a surprise to either of us that our approach had been much different. It is my personality to see the job that needs to be done and do it. I will do my best, but I am quick to admit that patience is not my strength. John, on the other hand, is a deliberative soul. He wants things just so before he ever begins a project. He labored out in that dirt preparing it for the plants. He broke up all the clumps, smoothed out the surface, spaced his plants the same distance, and watered them. He did everything in his power to make the soil a place where these plants would thrive and grow quickly.

I pondered this whole process for a couple of days. John and I both knew there was a lesson in our bunks somewhere. At first, I was certain his way was the best. I mean, honestly, you can't compete with soil that has been prepared and time that has been invested in advance. (You can see where this lesson could have gone towards building relationships and preparing to share the Gospel with others.) However, the more I've thought about it, I can see John's approach was best for John. It's what I love about him. He takes his time. He plans his approach. He prepares for what he is going to do and then he successfully completes what he sets out to do. However,

John's approach is not what is best for me. I am a free spirit. I usually wait to be inspired by something and then create it. As I have the urge to plant tomatoes, I want to do it. I figure I can break up the clumps and add the fertilizer later. (Just saying, I've now done both.) But it was more important to me at that moment to get my plants in the ground so they could be watered.) The bottom line is that neither approach was the "right" one. There was no right or wrong. There was his way and my way. We will need to wait until the plants grow to see if one thrives over the other. I suspect they will both flourish. Why? Because we aren't going to quit caring for them once they're in the ground. The caretaking has just begun. What John does in advance, I will do later. But we will both do eventually.

God was very clear in Jeremiah 29:11 when He said, "I know the plans I have for you, declares the Lord, plans to prosper you and not to harm you, plans to give you a hope and a future." The Scripture is written for John and for me. It is written for you, too. God's way of prospering me may look much different than John's. (Although considering we're married, some of our end results may be the same.) God told us in Jeremiah 1:5 that He knew us before we were born. He knew us before He even formed us in our mother's womb. Isn't that a little mind blowing? How do you know someone before they are even formed? I can't wait to find out the full extent of what God meant when I arrive in heaven. But I do know if He knew me before I was born, He is the One who created me to be more of a feeler than a thinker. If I tried to be someone other than whom God created me to be, I would be disobedient. I would be unfulfilled. I would not be living up to the potential God had created in me. While it is challenging for me to remember this at times, it is just as challenging to remember God made John to be who he is also. I don't want him to conform to my idea of who he should be or how he should act. And I trust he feels the same.

The bottom line here, stop trying to make comparisons between yourself and others. You have no idea what God's plan is for their life. If you have concerns about someone, pray for them. If you are comparing to convince yourself you're okay, well take that to the throne of heaven. I promise you God is waiting to deal with it. He wants you to know how loved you are. He did NOT make a mistake when He made you the way He did. There is someone you can connect with and minister to that someone else is not equipped to. You are not a failure. You are not a mistake. You are not a mess. You are a child of the most high God. You are created in His image. You are loved. Just. The. Way. You. Are. Embrace who He has created you to be. Seek His face and ask what His plans are for your life. The more you can accept who He created you to be, the more you will be able to surrender to His heart of love. Trust Him. He made you in His image, and you're just right. His love will make any changes that need to be made. You get to rest and rejoice that your Dad loves you so much He knew you BEFORE He even created you in your mother's womb. Let that sink in just a bit because it is truly amazing!

DISAPPOINTMENT

A couple of years ago, the preschool where I work was going to have a float in the local parade. The parade is held annually and that year we wanted to go all out. We had planned the theme for months creating class t-shirts and float decor to coordinate. As we got together the morning of the parade to begin assembly, can you guess what happened? Oh yes, a little rain shower came through. A rain shower, really? We weren't going to let that stop us! We worked all morning and at last were ready. There was glitter everywhere. (Those who love glitter can just envision the beauty! Those of you who are not quite as enthused about glitter, I'm sorry.) You can guess what happened, can't you? The "little rain shower" turned into a full-fledged all-out storm. And you guessed it. We didn't get to have the parade! Ugh! My response was certainly not a shining example of "Letting My Light Shine!" (The theme of the float.) But it raises an interesting question in my mind. What do you do with disappointment?

We've all experienced it before and will quite likely experience it again. We don't always get what we want or deserve and thus disappointment comes a calling. Is it wrong to be disappointed? No, I can't imagine it is. Is it wrong to wallow in it? Talk to it? Embrace it? Build on a room so it can live with you for a while? Yes, I'd say that crosses the line. Did Jesus have disappointments? How did He handle them?

I wish I could hear your feedback on things that you think may have been disappointing to Jesus. The obvious one that pops into my mind is His own death. The very people He loved and cared about decided to crucify Him. They whipped Him, spit on HIm, divided up His clothing, made Him carry His own cross, and hung Him on a tree to die. And what was His response? "Father, forgive them, for they know not what they are doing. (Luke 23:34)" "Truly I tell you, today you will be with me in paradise. (Luke 23:43)" And, "Father, into your hands I commit my spirit. (Luke 23:46)"

There are times when we are disappointed when we just need to let it go. The parade would be a good example of a "let it go" moment. It was not a big deal. But what about those situations that are big deals? When they were dividing up His clothes, Jesus went to the prayer asking for the forgiveness of those involved. Isn't that amazing? Look what they were doing to Him, and He stood before the Father and asked Him to forgive them. I want that kind of heart, but truth be told, I don't really want to have that kind of suffering. And oftentimes they go hand in hand. We learn to forgive through the moments of pain. It's hard to learn something if you never walk through it to experience it. Yet Jesus handled the situation by forgiving, which tells me we should, too.

I believe there are those times with disappointment when we have to just commit our spirit to the Lord. We may not get to know why we experienced certain disappointments. Why didn't you get the job you'd hoped for? Or what about the house you wanted but didn't get? Or even the birthday someone we love forgot? Disappointment comes in all shapes and sizes. Sometimes we may not ever get to know the reason for the disappointment. But we can always trust the hand of the One Who is in control of our lives. He loves us. He is for us. What looks like a great thing may end up being an awful thing. What looks awful may end up being what brings someone we love (or don't even know) to the Lord. It is an opportunity to "Trust in the Lord with all your heart and lean not on your own understanding; In all your ways submit to Him, and He will make your paths straight. (Proverbs 3:5-6)"

Jesus spent a great deal of time with His Dad. He often went off alone to pray. As we spend more time in the presence of the Father, we'll be much better prepared to handle life's disappointments. Right before His death, Jesus took His friends to the garden to pray. He was prayed up in advance. And He prayed His way through it. Let's follow His lead. Prayer and trust in the One Who loves you and created you with a purpose.

FEAR

D o you ever sit in your house and actually listen to the noises? It's strange how I can go about my day and not even hear the dryer banging (no shoes either!), the washing machine filling, the air conditioner kick on, the water heater refilling, etc. It's all there, part of the day, but it's noise I've become so accustomed to that I don't even consciously hear it.

But there are those nights when everyone is gone, and I'm home alone. I don't understand it, but then I can hear everything! The wind knocking something over on the deck, the refrigerator squeaking, the rocking chair making an odd sound. I love being alone (for a while), especially if I've worked all day and just need some down time, but I confess there must be a part of me that battles fear in the quiet.

Am I alone? Does anyone else experience those fears? What about the other fears you don't really share or tell anyone about? The fear of not being quite good enough? The fear that others will read your mind and know what you really think? The fear of being rejected? Abandoned? Or worse yet, being seen?

Adam and Eve were completely open and exposed to God. They walked with Him in the garden every day. He knew them. They were full of peace, joy, and happiness. And Love. He had given them everything they needed, and they got to walk with Him. Fully accepted. However, when Satan deceived Adam and Eve, what was the first thing they did? They hid themselves. Why? Why would they hide from the God who loved them? Because they knew they were naked. They were ashamed.

In our sin, we try to hide. We want to cover parts of ourselves so God doesn't see them. In fact, sometimes we even busy ourselves so we don't have to see them either. Yet, what would happen if we ran to the Light instead of covering ourselves from it? What if we came out from among the trees and asked God to forgive us? Help us? Change us? What if we told Him the truth? What if we told ourselves the truth? What if we admitted some of our habits may be a result of our fears?

Scripture says, "There is no fear in love. But perfect love drives out fear, because fear has to do with punishment. The one who fears is not made perfect in love. (1 John 4: 18)" Don't hide from the very thing that can help you. Rather don't hide from the One that can help you. Be open. Be exposed. Be real. God will heal the hurts, the brokenness, the fear. You just have to ask!

GLITTER AND DIRT

I came in from mowing today knowing I was covered with dirt and grass. I could feel the grit and grime. I also smelled like apple juice after mowing over several apples that had fallen off the apple tree. (Not a recommended strategy for mowing.) I had juice dripping from my glasses and covering my legs. I can't wait to eat one of the apples because clearly, they are very juicy!

As I looked in the mirror while washing my hands, I noticed I was sparkling. I had to chuckle. I'd been adding glitter to a bulletin board at school yesterday and brought some of the "bottled sunshine" home with me. Well, you can't beat that now, can you? Dirt and glitter. A girl's best friends! It reminded me of a t-shirt a student had given me last year. It said, "I love glitter and mud!"

Dirt and glitter. What could they possibly have to do with Jesus? The dirt could represent so many things. But today it reminded me of something sobering to remember. The battle is dirty. As you follow Jesus, it's not always going to feel like sunshine and rainbows. Oh, the joy of Jesus is constant. He will never change. But as you dig in and begin investing in people's lives, as you follow Jesus wherever He leads, be prepared that it might get a little messy. Because people are messy. I have yet to meet anyone other than Jesus who is perfect. It therefore stands to reason that building relationships is going to take work. There will be ups and downs. Joys and sadness. Hurts and forgiveness. You're going to experience the mess. Yet, the end result is very worthwhile. It's the glitter. The sparkle added to your world by sticking with someone through thick and thin. You'll get to experience your own growth as a person as well as watch what the commitment of loving someone the way Jesus does can do!

Did I mention that how someone else behaves does not get to dictate our behavior? We are responsible to be the person God calls us to be. I don't want my behavior to become dependent upon circumstances or how I'm treated. I need to respond each time like Jesus would. What do I mean by that? If someone is rude, I can choose to be polite. (Luke 6:28) Jesus would want that of me. If someone is angry, I can respond softly and kindly. (Proverbs 15:1) We will not be judged by someone else's behavior; we each answer to God individually. (2 Corinthians 5:10) Besides, we're often filtering other's behavior through our own baggage. It takes all the guesswork out when you respond in the Spirit.

As I close, please keep in mind, I haven't mastered the dirt yet. As I write these devotions, God is speaking more to me than anyone else. But I 100 per cent believe the glitter is worth the dirt! The glitter wouldn't mean a thing without it!

"Love the Lord your God with all your heart and with all your soul and with all your mind and with all your strength. The second is this: Love your neighbor as yourself. There is no commandment greater than these. (Mark 12: 30-31)"

BROKEN LEADER

As I was out mowing today, I caught the edge of a smaller evergreen. By smaller, I'd say it was just a foot or two taller than me. I heard a bit of a grind, so I figured I'd caught one of the lower branches. I cringed and was once again thankful John wasn't close enough to give me a talking to. I made the loop around the lawn, and as I approached the tree again, I noticed the top was missing. Uh oh! How could that be? Surely, I had not hit the tree hard enough to somehow pull the top off!

Upon closer inspection, I realized that I had not broken the top off the tree, but instead it appeared the leader had died out a while ago. (The leader on a tree is the branch which vertically runs up the center and will become the trunk which all other branches grow from.) Strange. I'd mowed that yard all summer, and I'd never even noticed it. It wasn't until I thought I'd hurt the tree, that I noticed it was already broken.

How often do you accidentally hurt someone's feelings? Perhaps you use sarcasm, and it's not well received. Have you neglected to include them? Not connected with their emotions in a way they needed you to? And, it isn't until their reaction of severe pain, that you notice the brokenness. They were already walking around broken, and you just never looked close enough to see it. We get so busy doing the next thing or are preoccupied with our own lives, that we can interact with people on a daily basis who are crying out for help and never even notice. They may hide it well, just as the tree had from me. I didn't even see part of it had died. It wasn't until I heard the clunk that I looked deeper and realized it.

You may be the only hope someone knows today. We don't know the extent of the pain people carry around. The hurt. The parts of themselves which they feel have died. But God can use you to be part of their solution. Reach out to someone today. Show them they are loved. Love them not with your love but the love of Jesus. Let them know they are accepted just the way they are. Did they overreact, and you took the brunt of it? Praise Jesus! He's showing you they need you. No, they need Him in you. You won't be able to fix them. You can't change them. But you can most certainly love them. Point them to the cross. Where the Savior demonstrated the extent of His great love for us. Help them to realize that there is Someone who can bring hope and healing. Someone who wants to change their lives. Someone who will take what feels broken and dead and breathe life into it. Remember, you may be walking right by that person every day. You may work with them. Go to school with them. They may be in your front yard, and you have driven by them all summer just like our tree. And you did not see their pain. Oh, they may think they are hiding it well. Listen to the Spirit. He will guide you and point you to those who need hope.

"A new command I give you: Love one another. As I have loved you, so you must love one another. By this everyone will know that you are my disciples, if you love one another. (John 13:34-35)"

SPRAYING WEEDS AGAIN

Yesterday was a perfect Iowa day to be outside. I appreciated that I could be home all day and enjoy mowing the yard and tackling the flower beds. In between all the activities, my friend called. I told her I was getting ready to finish up the mowing and needed to go spray my weeds. She said, "It seems like the last several times we've talked, you've been ready to go spray your weeds."

Hmm, I had to think about that one. It's quite likely true. The farm we live on has lots of space, and I love flowers. I was introduced several years ago to the notion of spraying all the grass and weeds that come up rather than attempt to pull them. I'm not condoning it as the healthiest choice, but definitely the easiest.

Once John got home, I told him I had used the big sprayer in the garage specifically marked for weeds and hoped that's what was really in the jug. His response, "It probably won't work. If you don't spray the same day you mix it up, it hasn't been working right and seems to lose its potency." Ugh! Well, I have no choice other than to wait a few days. If it doesn't work, I'll go back out and do it again.

As I pondered my friend's comment, something about it seemed to keep stirring in my spirit. I knew God had a lesson to teach me. First, it's true. I am frequently going out to deal with the weeds in my yard. No matter how many weeds you pull or spray, they just keep coming. And I've discovered even once they die, you sometimes **still** have to pull them, or they just look dead and ugly. (But at least you've gotten the root.) Also, I have to be super careful, because if I hit the flowers with the spray, they, too, will die.

Isn't it the same in our lives? Mark 4:7 "Other seed fell among thorns, which grew up and choked the plants, so that they did not bear grain." As I was looking for that Scripture, I came across a parable I don't remember ever hearing before. Matthew 13:24-30 shares about an enemy who went and threw weed seed in among a farmer's wheat. (Side note: That would REALLY irritate me if someone purposely threw weed seed in my yard!) As it began to come up, the workers discovered there were weeds and grain growing together. They wanted to know whether they should pull it, but the farmer indicated they needed to wait until both the weeds and the wheat were both fully grown. If they pulled the weeds too soon, they may accidentally take the wheat with it. "Let both grow together until the harvest. At that time, I will tell the harvesters: First collect the weeds and tie them in bundles to be burned; then gather the wheat and bring it into my barn.'"

Weeds in our life need to be dealt with. As the Lord reveals weeds in your life, take them to the throne and ask Him to remove them. I hope and pray you don't have any; but in all reality, I suspect you do. Because, sadly, we also have an enemy. And he is going to attempt to steal and destroy all the good seed that gets planted. God wants to remove those weeds by their roots. My experience with letting weeds get pulled in my life is varied. Sometimes the weeds are little and come right out with ease. But there are other times when I've been carrying around sin and unhealthy coping skills since I was a child. Those tend to have deeper roots. The extraction process is not always painless. But the freedom that comes from removing the weeds is priceless.

What qualifies as a weed? According to Matthew 13:22 it's worry and the deceitfulness of wealth. But could weeds look differently? Maybe it's an addiction? Giving in to loneliness. Self-pity? Competitiveness in unhealthy situations? Comparison? Envy? Wow, who knew there was such a wide variety of weeds? If we want the full beauty of the healthy flower to bloom, we may need to surrender to the pulling of the weeds. And, if they return, you may need more than one dose of weed killer to get rid of them.

There is only true freedom in Jesus. He came to set us free, and we are free indeed. The process of sanctification may not always be easy, but it is always worth it. Holding on to the lie that what the world has to offer is more fulfilling than Jesus will only fertilize what you don't want to grow. Surrender. Trust Him. Stay in the Word of God and let it come alive in you. If you don't feel you're understanding what you read, ask the Holy Spirit to bring it to life. He will. I guarantee it's something He WANTS to happen. The Word and the Spirit will kill those unwanted weeds! He's just waiting to be asked.

Blessings! Enjoy your time with Jesus today!

GET THE ROOT

Y ou would be surprised by all the lessons that can be
learned while mowing a cemetery. I was astounded by
all the teaching moments available while riding around
on a lawnmower.

One of the things I noticed today was the sign over the cemetery
and the rock landscaping underneath it. I recalled that last week I
had to raise up the deck to mow over the rocks, because there were
weeds that were growing abundantly beneath the sign. (Deck raised
to save the blades.) Today, the weeds were again thriving. Of course,
we've had some rain, and this assisted in their rapid growth, but
don't you find it fascinating that weeds grow in any weather? But
even more curious to me is the fact that I never see thick luscious
grass popping up in these random type places. Here is an area which
should be all rock but the weeds flourish. In fact, they flourish to the
point where you can't even see the rocks until you cut the weeds or
kill them.

It brought a rather challenging topic to mind and one that is
never fun to have to look at. Bitterness and unforgiveness. Have you
ever noticed that when you're carrying around unforgiveness that
bitterness seems to flourish? Hebrews 12:15 says, "See to it that no
one falls short of the grace of God and that no bitter root grows up

to cause trouble and defile many." The harder your heart (rocks) becomes, the more rampant the bitterness (weeds) begins to pop up. And just like a pig weed doesn't mind growing next to a button weed, bitterness doesn't grow alone either. You know jealousy and envy are always eager to hop on the unforgiveness train. What about that unhealthy competitiveness that will come knocking? And unforgiveness sows a critical spirit like no other. Weeds. All spiritual weeds. And they flourish in the hard heart of unforgiveness. And just like the weeds at the cemetery, if you water them, they will grow even more. You can have a whole little garden of nastiness and sin before it's all said and done. Let me tell you, just like the weeds are a pain in the ying yang, unforgiveness is equally as unattractive. If you think you can hide it, you are mistaken. Our cemetery has a great big sign announcing the location right at the entrance. However, it is completely overshadowed, because your eye is instantly drawn to the weeds! That's the trouble with unforgiveness, too. Its roots and weeds begin to overtake your personality, and pretty soon it becomes how people define you. Not attractive to say the least and almost impossible to hide.

Here's the great news though! God doesn't define you by bitterness, but He does want you to walk in freedom from it. "If we confess our sins, he is faithful and just and will forgive us our sins and purify us from all unrighteousness. (1 John 1:9)" If you confess to the Lord that you are feeling bitter, He will empower you to release it and walk in forgiveness. It doesn't mean your hurt wasn't real. It just means you are handing over the consequences of someone else's behavior (or maybe your own poor choice) to the Lord. Romans 12:9 tells us not to "…take revenge, my dear friends, but leave room for God's wrath, for it is written: 'It is mine to avenge; I will repay, says the Lord.;" God will take care of the vengeance. He wants you to walk in faith and trust. You can trust His love for you and know He will deal with your pain. Oh, and just so you know, you're not alone. I want to give you a "heads up." The bitterness might try to come knocking again. Last week I mowed all those weeds off and here they were all back again today. John didn't mow them this time. He said he's going to spray them. Apparently, a full size weed is easier to kill with the spray, because the leaves will assist in the absorption and go to the root of the plant to kill it. (Hmm, I learned something new today. Did you know this?) You may need to stand on the promises of Scripture if you are tempted to return to the offense. Just speak it out loud, "Nope, I've forgiven that. Lord, it's yours to deal with." (Different devotional, but God spoke the world into creation and His Spirit lives inside you. Therefore, your speaking of His Word out loud has power.) As you spray that unforgiveness with God's unconditional love and the Word, it will carry truth clear to the root of the issue (often unbelief aka not trusting that God loves you just the way you are, which is the reason we get offended in the first place). The root will die, but you will live!

"For to me, to live is Christ and to die is gain. (Philippians 1:21)"

GOD IS
STILL GOOD

O ur car has one of those back-up cameras. I don't know about you, but I almost get motion sickness trying to use the thing. For the first two months we owned the vehicle, I **didn't** use it. But now with a puppy to watch out for and seeing John utilize it, I've decided I may as well give it a try. As it turns out, I am finding it to be rather handy. However, a morning like today led to some deeper thinking.

You see, we live on a gravel road. As a result, the back window of the Equinox was so dirty that I wasn't able to see much of anything. I put the wipers on which helped some, but it was "clear" (ha! play on words, thank you very much) that it wasn't going to fully resolve the problem. There must have been dirt on the camera. As I headed down the road for work, I just knew God was telling me something, but what was it?

How often do we begin to rely on something which may not give the clarity we need? Just as the camera had been offering what appeared to be a convenient and clear path of what was behind me, it had become dirty and therefore not effective. The view was distorted and unclear. Going backwards, as I trusted the obscured view on the video, was proving to be a bit dangerous. I could have gotten out and found the location of the camera and cleaned it up a bit, but I didn't take the time to do that little task. My question to you today is are you looking backwards or forward? My vision would have been clear if I had been driving forward. But not backwards. And if I didn't use the video and instead tried the rearview mirror it was still unhelpful because of that same dirt. Do you spend time looking in your rearview mirror? Are you focusing your thoughts and energy on something behind you cannot undo? Perhaps you have regrets? Wish you had made different choices? Or, now that you're in the present looking back it isn't quite as clear. It's difficult to make out what's back there because it's through the lens of the present. Or the lens of hurt? Pain? Regret? Or perhaps even a rosy colored perception of a non-reality. Regardless of your answer, I want you to know today that whether your past is filled with love and joy or regrets and guilt, God was God then and He is still God today. He loves you and has forgiveness awaiting your acceptance. It's there. It's for you. Whether what's in your past is dirty or clean, He was still there. He was still loving you. He was still protecting you. He was and is still good. It's His character. He cannot be anything but good. It's who He is.

This brings me to my next and last question. We know who God is. He is God. He is good. He is love. He is peace. He is loyal, trustworthy, kind, gentle, and forgiving. But who are you? In the light of knowing who Christ is, does it change you? Are you willing to open your heart and fully surrender it to Him? Can you turn off your camera that blurs the images of what's behind you and keep your eyes on today? Will you trust Him to take your sins past and present and forgive them? To hold you, comfort you, and restore you in areas you felt had no hope? I hope you will choose today to fix your eyes Up rather than back. And, if you need to take a quick glimpse back there, maybe for healing and restoration, be sure to clean the camera so the picture you are seeing is clear. You want to see it through the eyes of Jesus. Not the eyes of falsehoods or shame. "Let us **fix our eyes on Jesus**, **the** author and perfecter **of our** faith, who for **the** joy set before him endured **the** cross, scorning its shame, and sat down at **the** right hand **of the** throne **of** God. (Hebrews 12:2)" "Therefore, there is now no condemnation for those who are in Christ Jesus. (Romans 8:1)"

MORE THAN WE ASK, THINK, OR EVEN IMAGINE

The school ran out of black construction paper last week. I went online, placed the order, and hoped it would arrive prior to the next craft which would require its use. Yesterday I noticed a large (and I mean large), flat package outside the office door. I stopped to read the name and was surprised it was mine. I picked it up and was a bit taken aback by its weight. I had no idea what it could be, because it was certainly not the size of three packages of black construction paper. OH, MY GOODNESS! I opened the package to discover two **gigantic** packages of black paper. Our 8 ½ x 11 had just become 2 ft x 3 ft. I'd love to say they made the error, but I'm not always the best "details person," so it was quite likely my fault. I burst out laughing. What on earth we are going to do with the paper other than cut it down, I'm not sure. But I do find it a wee bit hilarious!

The great thing about this error was the lesson which came with it. How often do we ask God for something we need? We go to Him with an 8 ½ x 11 request and He delivers a 2 ft x 3 ft answer. Ephesians 3:20 tell us that God is able to do "immeasurably more than all we ask or imagine, according to His power that is at work within us...." How often do we go to the Father with what we think we need or want only to discover that His answer is filled with so much more? Don't you love the verse in James which tells us "ye have not, because ye ask not?" Does it make you want to close your eyes, ask God to forgive you for your lack of faith, and pray that He shows you what to ask for and pray about. Don't you want all that God wants to give? More than you can even imagine? And just think, according to the end of Ephesians 3 it is His power at work within you. The power of God lives in you! You have access to Him all the time. He isn't randomly coming and going based upon His mood. He is a permanent resident inside His children who love Him. He is waiting to give you more than you can think or imagine.

Part of our routine in preschool is to have a daily "prayer." The prayer of the day gets to place a sticker on the map of the United States. Wherever the sticker is placed is the state and people we pray for. Last week the children asked God to bless a family in Maine. Today they went to the throne on behalf of a widow. It is always a blessing to watch those who are new to praying and a bit hesitant learn to talk to God about their needs and desires. We try to pray for our friends and teachers when they're gone, or any pressing need the students may share. I pray the children will grow into prayer warriors who go to God and ask for big things. I don't want them to have not because they ask not. If they're angry, we teach them to stop and pray. If they're hurting, we can model friends taking us to Jesus when we can't take ourselves. If they're excited about something, a "Praise God! He is amazing!" is a great impromptu prayer of thanksgiving. If the children can learn a lifestyle of prayer, they will be armed and empowered to walk in victory along with a moment-by-moment relationship of talking with Jesus.

Keep in mind, you are God's child. You are His treasure. He hears you pray (engage in a relationship with Him), and he responds just the way a loving earthly father does when his child is in need.

He comforts. He gives. He loves. He hears you, loves you, and is waiting to sit down for a chat. You'll be surprised at the perspective He offers, and the answers He delivers. Take a moment today and hang out with your heavenly Dad. And wait expectantly for the incredible response He intends to bring.

YOUR FOOD
SOURCE

One day I was reading a book about Helen Keller with a student. Helen was born a healthy child who could both see and hear. However, after a bout with illness, she lost the use of both of those senses. She had demonstrated that she was a bright child but because of her inability to see or hear, her family tended to give her whatever she wanted. Apparently, the use of the word "no" led to major temper tantrums. If you've ever engaged with someone who hasn't heard the word very often, you can likely envision what the meltdown looks like when it's used. While there is no actual harm being done to the person, they carry on in such a way that you'd think their hair was on fire.

Helen's life changed when her family hired a teacher named Annie Sullivan. Annie realized immediately that there were going to be fundamental challenges to overcome before learning could even begin. In a sense, Helen was going to need to die to self (her old ways of coping) in order to rise into who God intended her to be. Helen needed to learn self-control and how to effectively communicate without a tantrum. I think the beginning of Annie's employment was captured well in the line in the book that said, "The war was on..."

As the student and I were reading the book together, we were talking about the part of Annie's arrival when she made Helen sit down and eat using a spoon. Helen threw the spoon to the floor. Annie made her pick it up. Helen continued the behavior until she realized she would need to use the spoon if she wanted to eat. The days in her life of eating off the plates of others were over. I've got to stop here because a big revelation just jumped off the page. Did you catch it? Helen used to just wander around the table and eat other people's food right off their plate. Why? Because people saw her inability to see and hear rather than her potential to eat from the table. I'm curious. Have you been spiritually eating off the plates of other believers or feeding yourself? If you are gaining your spiritual food strictly from other believers' plates, I'd encourage you to open your heart and let the Spirit really begin to move and speak. God wants a personal relationship with you. You are important to Him. You are created with a special purpose. He does not look at you and see a child who is unable to see or hear. Oh, no, He sees a child who is quite capable of sitting at the table. He has the food all prepared. He is waiting to nourish you through His Word, sermons, fellowship with other believers and the multiple other ways He chooses to speak. Are you willing to sit down and listen? He has given you all the skills necessary to feed yourself (His Spirit will assist). Are you throwing down your spoon, because you don't want to change how you've been doing things? Are you carrying bitterness towards the church or perhaps another person? Hmm, might you be having a little spiritual temper tantrum? Is it easier to use the excuse to avoid engagement with Jesus rather than "pick up the spoon" and allow God to heal, feed, and restore?

The most interesting part of my interaction with the student came after reading about the spoon. The student looked at me and asked what would happen if they threw the book across the room? I said, "I'd make you go pick it up." Response, "Well, just because you're bigger than me doesn't mean you could make me do it." Me,

"I wouldn't make you pick it up because I'm bigger than you. I'd make you pick it up, because I've been given the authority in this situation." Oh, my gracious! I heard those words come out of my mouth, and the Spirit in me about knocked me out of the chair. "Leslie, do you hear yourself?" You have been given authority! And if I have it, you have it too!

It says in 1 Corinthians 6:19 that "...your bodies are temples of the Holy Spirit, who is in you, whom you have received from God? You are not your own;..." and Luke 10:19 "I have given you authority to trample on snakes and scorpions and to overcome all the power of the enemy; nothing will harm you." We have authority! God has given you power over all those distractions, excuses, and sins which are attempting to prevent you from growing and learning and walking with Jesus. Just as Annie was given authority over Helen, you have been given authority over the enemy. God said it clearly in His Word. Thankfully, God does not lie. So, my next question to you is this. Are you walking in it? Annie Sullivan was given authority over Helen, but she had to own it. She could have let Helen continue to throw fits and get her way. She didn't allow it because she knew Helen was created for more. You are not a victim. God has designed you for more. He knows the plans He has for you, and they are to prosper you and not to harm you. (Jeremiah 29:11) I want to encourage you today to dig into the Word. See what God has to say about you. And start believing Him! You have the authority to walk in freedom and victory. You are not a helpless child running around begging food from other people's plates. Oh, no! You are a victor! You can sit at the table and eat with the King of kings. Do not allow yourself to be defined by who the world says you are. You are a child of God who created the heavens and the earth. Let THAT Truth define your behavior, choices, and decision-making. You are a loved child of the most Holy of holies. You are already loved. He wants the absolute best for you. As we walk in obedience, it's not about following a bunch of rules. It's about trusting that God is for me and wants the best for me. If He tells me to do something, it will be for my best. He's not piling on a bunch of rules and expecting us to figure out how to successfully complete the tasks. Oh, no. When God showed us His will, He filled us with His Holy Spirit. The Spirit will empower us to walk in victory. Your Dad loves you! Enjoy your time with Him. Spending time with you is one of His very favorite activities. I'm convinced of it!

IT'S NOT UNDERWEAR

If you want a true test of your self-perception, all you need to do is work with children. One of the things I love about kids is that they are honest. I'm not sure when we adapt the concept that being careful not to hurt someone's feelings is more important than telling them the truth, but most children do not view life through the lens of this filter.

The other day, I was wearing a pair of distressed shorts that had a daisy print behind them. I love these shorts! I encountered a student who saw me and said, "Teacher, I can see your underwear!"

Sigh. "No, that's not my underwear." (It was a cute navy print covered in little daisies.)

"Yes," she was convinced it was my underwear.

"No, it isn't my underwear."

Fast forward two days and this same child looks at me (mind you, she should be reading her story) and says, "Teacher, your shirt is dirty."

Sigh. "No, my shirt is not dirty. It is tie-dyed brown."

"Well, it looks dirty."

Great, I now have my favorite shorts that give the presentation of underwear, and my fun tie-dyed shirt that looks dirty. Be strong, Leslie. Be strong!

Oh, we can't end with my clothing. Yesterday, I was taking a turn reading when I felt myself being examined. I suspect nothing I said was being heard, because I was no more than finished reading when I heard, "What happened to your teeth?"

(Oh, my goodness! I almost died laughing!) "What do you mean?" I suspected I knew what they were asking, but why not make them say it. Maybe I had imperfections I wasn't aware of yet.

"On the bottom, what's wrong with them?"

I responded, "They're crooked."

Of course, the child wants to know, "Why?"

"I don't know, it's the way God put them in my mouth. They didn't used to be that crooked but as I get older, they are getting worse." Now after twenty plus years of working with children, I am not the least bit offended by these types of comments. It was not a shock to me that my bottom teeth were crooked nor the first time I've been asked about them. However, I absolutely LOVED where the conversation took a turn.

This student was offering a solution. "Won't braces help?"

Too funny! "Yes, I am sure they would, but I'm in my fifties and just don't know if I want to deal with braces. I think it would be a lot of pain for my mouth all the time."

Now wait for it. "Have you thought about Invisalign?" I burst out laughing and the poor child smirks and tells me they're just trying to help come up with a solution. You just have to love children!

Just to be clear, I have thought about getting braces to correct my crooked bottom teeth. However, I do anticipate it would hurt like a bugger, and my body really doesn't need to have something stuck in it promoting inflammation. But do you know what's completely amazing about each one of these interactions? I never once felt unloved. As I was being questioned about my shorts showing my underwear, I was holding the beautiful flowers this child had picked for me. How could I feel anything but loved? And really, how sweet was it for someone to gently ask what happened to my teeth and then offer up suggestions to resolve what they perceived as an issue?

We live in a world that often does not like to tell the truth if it is going to hurt someone's feelings. Even worse, we hear news reports in which the truth seems to be made up, skewed, or completely non-existent. How do we know the truth, and what are we supposed to do with it when we hear it? Well, regardless of what people may try and lead you to believe, there is only one Truth. Jesus said in Scripture, "I am the Way, the Truth, and the Life." If you're in doubt about what you're hearing, the Word will tell you the absolute truth. God wrote the Word for this very purpose. He loves you and wants you to know what is true, and what isn't true. If what you are hearing does not line up with the Word of God, it isn't true. And just like when the little girl wanted me to know she could see my underwear, (Remember, this was NOT true. No underwear was visible.) it didn't mean she didn't love me. After all, I was holding the gift of fresh picked flowers she brought BECAUSE she loves me. Just because the Word clearly speaks to something being a sin, it doesn't mean God doesn't love us. Romans 8:38 tells us that "...nothing can separate us from the love of God that is revealed in Christ Jesus our Lord." However, it is important that we are willing and able to hear God's Truth and receive it. It's how we can heal, grow, and allow Him to change us. If we can't see the sin, we can't see our need for a Savior.

It is imperative that we realize God's love is not dependent upon our perfection or performance. He isn't collecting a data sheet filled with notes regarding each time we mess up (or succeed for that matter). As we make mistakes, He's calling us back to Himself. He hates sin, because He loves us. He doesn't want anything to stand between us and Him. He wants us to avoid hurt and pain. Jesus has paid the price for our sin. Once you have received Jesus as your personal Savior, He resides inside you. As I make mistakes, I am free to come to the Father and say, "I'm so sorry!" You know what God does? He looks at me. Hears me. Sees Jesus in me and reminds me that I'm forgiven and loved. Jesus paid the price already. I'm covered. Avoiding God because I'm afraid of His response is hurting me. (Because then I don't get the reassurance of my Dad.) But it has to make God sad when we don't come to see Him, too. As much as I **don't** want to know when I've sinned, I **do** want to know when I've sinned. After all, "If we confess our sins, He is faithful and just to forgive our sins and purify us from all unrighteousness. (1 John 1:9)"

A NEW PERSPECTIVE

I was out enjoying the evening on the lawn mower last night. There were two sections of lawn which hadn't been touched since vacation, and it was FUN! If you live on a farm, you know what I mean. It's the stage where the grass has actually gotten to be way too tall, and you think the best option might be to just let the sheep eat it off. (No, we don't actually have sheep. But, if we did, it was at that stage.) However, it's also the stage where it's obvious you have done something when you're finished. The difference between the tall grass and the freshly mowed grass is so distinct that it makes your heart sing a little song.

If you're tracking what I'm talking about, perhaps you'll also understand the REALLY tall grass under the trees. You know the ones. They are the ones where the branches are just too low, and you can't quite get under. (If you've read my other devotions, you know the ones. The ones where you smack your head when you're not paying close enough attention.) They aren't just sporting a couple of weeks of "behind mowing," but maybe three or four weeks' worth. Because, if you don't go get the weed eater, you're never going to get under there and get it all.

Last night, I ended up mowing the opposite direction than I usually do. I'm one of those boring mowers who usually goes the same way. You know, you have to spray the grass away from the flower beds the first time or two around, and then you can turn and go the other way so the grass doesn't make windrows in the middle when you're all done. Well, for some reason, I kept going the opposite direction. And you know what was strange? I managed to get under the two difficult trees. It's like the gates of heaven opened up, and there was a big opening which the mower fit into perfectly. (Of course, there is still a pretty good space RIGHT next to the tree I couldn't get, but that's a different devotional.)

Why? Why was I able to see the gap last night and not every other time I've mowed this summer? Was the gap not there before? No. It was there the entire time. I had just never approached it from that direction before. I had not seen the opening until I came at the tree from a different angle. I was now able to see the tree from a new perspective.

It makes me think of Paul. There he was persecuting Christians. (Acts 9:1-2, 1 Corinthians 15:9) He was raised as a Pharisee. He was well educated. But he didn't understand the message of salvation. He hadn't understood the need for and importance of a personal relationship with Jesus. He had not yet received it down in his heart. His spirit. Where it would change his life and his eternity. However, Paul's life was changed when God met him on the road to Damascus. When He spoke to him. When Paul lost his sight. When God sent Ananias, and he was healed. (Acts 9:17) Paul had a new perspective. He could see the Truth! Just as I could see the opening while mowing, Paul could see Jesus. Paul had a new perspective.

He must have heard the message of Jesus, or it doesn't seem he would have been upset with the believers. Yet at first, he didn't "see" the way. The Way. Jesus says, "I am the Way and the Truth and the

168

life. No one comes to the Father except through me. (John 14:6)" Do you have an area of your life you aren't seeing change? Have the people closest to you mentioned something they are concerned with? Are you struggling with something only you know about and is impacting your walk with Christ? Ask God for a new perspective. Or if you are seeing something in others or have friends who don't know Jesus, ask God to give them a new perspective. "The Lord is not slow in keeping his promise, as some understand slowness. Instead, he is patient with you, not wanting anyone to perish, but everyone to come to repentance. (2 Peter 3:9)"

"And I am certain that God, who began the good work within you, will continue his work until it is finally finished on the day when Christ Jesus returns. (Philippians 1:6)" Blessings, Friends!

YELLOW PEONY

I sometimes think our front yard holds a Bible Study just waiting to be written. It could be titled Lessons Learned in the Front Yard. I was certain today's lesson would have to do with the beautiful choir of birds singing to me as I sat in the bright yellow chair on the deck. But nope. As I walked past the apple tree loaded with little apples awaiting their abundant harvest this fall, I noticed one little spot of dead leaves. Uh oh! Did we have trouble brewing?

How often do I see the three or four dead leaves in someone's life and zero in on those rather than focus on all the fruit God is growing in them? Gulp! Lawn lessons are hard! Dear Jesus, please change my heart to love like Yours!

Around the house, I go and spot the yellow peony tree in our backyard. Like the apple tree, it had spots that had died. Last year's had not yet been removed from inside the bush, and yet the beautiful yellow flowers were gorgeous. Which would I allow myself to dwell on? The life or the death?

What dead areas has God not yet removed from your life? Don't allow yourself to feel you can't be used by the Lord because you  aren't perfect. There may be parts of you that are still awaiting transformation. You may have parts dying to self as we speak. Yet, God graciously allows His beauty in the midst of the transforming process. I am so thankful for His unconditional love. His love will change what needs to be changed. Today, just focus on your love relationship and enjoy the beauty He created in you!

THE IRIS

Yesterday I was out working in the yard and came across this beauty. I don't know where we got her or how long we've had her, but I was struck by the intricate details of the flower. I can see this flower from the living room window and have enjoyed the burst of color by the swing set. However, as I went outside and got up close, there were so many features not visible from far away. The deep colors add a rich backdrop for the orange and pink tones and a closer look still reveals the pollen inside which will be enjoyed by the bees. It is a true reflection of God's artistic skills and His incredible love for us to take the time to create something this beautiful.

It made me wonder how many people we see from afar but never really take the time to get to know. We live lives that seem to be operating on high most of the time. We see people across the grocery store and wave, but how often do we stop and have a conversation. Those people at work who you aren't super enthused about, how well do you actually know them? Is it a situation like the living room window? Perhaps from across the room, they seem okay but nothing special. Let's face it, maybe they are even a tad bit annoying. What would happen if you got close up? What would happen if you began to be kind? Engage them in conversation? What might be the beauty you would discover once you got a closer look into their lives?

Here's the thing though. It's not just the "getting to know" people which struck me about the flower. It's the "getting to know" God. Are you viewing God through the window per se? You can see Him out there. Sure, He's okay. Just as the flower isn't making the scenery less attractive, does God seem good enough to have around as long as He stays over there? You might need Him at some point so it's good to keep Him visible. What would happen if you got a closer look? What might you discover if you allowed yourself to really stop and examine Who God is? I guarantee you'll discover there's more! God isn't just sitting upstairs on a throne watching things in your life play out. Oh, no, He's got such a depth and intricacy to His Personhood that we'll spend a lifetime getting to discover. What would happen if you took the time to really embrace Who He is? What if you "picked the flower" and brought it inside where you could enjoy it? What if you allowed God to become a part of your life on a daily basis? You would discover He is even more beautiful than the close-up of the flower.

There is something interesting about those irises. They used to be planted south of my mother-in-law's house. I would notice them as I drove in and out the lane but didn't often go over to appreciate them like I did yesterday. Last fall we took the house down, and the flowers needed to be relocated. I am thrilled that they are thriving near the swing set. Is it possible that some relocation needs to be taking place? Would you see God differently if you were viewing Him from a different perspective? Is it possible there is more to God than you've allowed yourself to discover? I'd encourage you to get into the Word and find out. I stand in awe today of who God is. I am amazed at how much more He reveals about Himself when I'm willing to listen. He WANTS to be connected. He WANTS a relationship with you. He WANTS you to know Him. He wants you to see His beauty, His power, His love, His extensive grace. You might need to relocate yourself so you can see Him more clearly. You might need to slow down your life a bit and make time for Him. You might need to spend more time in the Word to discover what He wants to tell you. Oh, trust me, once you get in there it's not going to be burdensome. The time you spend with the Father, His Son, and Holy Spirit will be the most precious time of your life. He is waiting. He's anxious to give you the victory you've been yearning to walk in. He wants you to see yourself through His lens. He wants you to know He is for you and not against you. The vastness of His love for us is something I'm not sure we'll ever fully discover.

This verse is one of my favorites. I apologize if I quote it a lot. Years ago, God laid it on my heart, and I've often prayed it for myself and others. It is from Ephesians. If you'd like to know Jesus more intimately, I would highly recommend praying this prayer daily if not several times a day. You can personalize it. If something is in the Word and you pray the Word, you know you are praying God's will. There is power in praying the Scriptures. Write it on a sticky note and pray it as you get ready for work. Put it on your dashboard so it's visible when you get in the car. Or sit on your deck and pray it softly as the birds are singing in the background. Watch as God uses His Word to begin to transform your life into one rooted and grounded in His love! He is life-changing!

"I pray that out of his glorious riches he may strengthen you with power through his Spirit in your inner being, so that Christ may dwell in your hearts through faith. And I pray that you, being rooted and established in love, may have power, together with all the Lord's holy people, to grasp how wide and long and high and deep is the love of Christ, and to know this love that surpasses knowledge—that you may be filled to the measure of all the fullness of God. Now to him who is able to do immeasurably more than all we ask or imagine, according to his power that is at work within us, to him be glory in the church and in Christ Jesus throughout all generations, for ever and ever! Amen. (Ephesians 3:16-21)"

WISTERIA

Years ago, I planted a wisteria vine next to one of the pillars leading down the path west of our house. Every year, I would get so excited because SURELY this would be the year it would bloom. I planted another vine on the other pillar and while it didn't have flowers, it was beautiful. I pruned. I sprayed the weeds (wondering if these were the ultimate culprit). But never any flowers. I decided I didn't have a clue how to grow a wisteria vine and gave up!

The picture shows the wisteria that bloomed full force on our dog kennel fence this year. I had NO idea what the vine was. I paid no attention to it. It has a tag so apparently, I planted it, but I have no idea when. And I only started looking for a tag because I didn't even know what the flower was. It turned out to be absolutely stunning.

I have no idea how many times I went out to look at these beautiful flowers, but they have brought me great joy. And guess what? I didn't really do anything other than plant the thing and apparently forgot I'd done it. (I was positive it was going to be a trumpet vine, because to John's great dismay they come up EVERYWHERE.) You know, just like the vines, we can pre-plan how we want to share Jesus with others. Oh, there isn't anything wrong with reaching out and loving others. We're wired for it. But the flowers offer a great reminder that no matter how much we plan and organize (or fret and stew and try to control), "Unless the LORD builds the house, the builders labor in vain. Unless the LORD watches over the city, the guards stand watch in vain. (Psalm 127:1)" I don't know about you, but I spend a lot of unnecessary energy because I try to pick up responsibilities which are not mine. They belong to Jesus. I have the joy of sharing Christ and planting seeds, but it's HIS job to grow them. We don't have the power to change hearts, but God does. We can make all the plans we want but ultimately the Lord determines the results. "The heart of man plans his way, but the Lord establishes his steps. Proverbs 16:9 You be who God created you to be and rejoice as the Holy Spirit does what He does!

WHAT SEASON
IS IT?

As I was driving to school today, I happened to notice the landscape scattered with big round hay bales. It was beautiful. There they were all tightly bound and awaiting relocation to a more convenient location where they could be used as feed during the cold winter months. As I soaked in the beauty of the moment, it struck me how unexpected the connection is to our faith walk.

The planting of the seed in the spring, the care of the land all summer to keep the weeds at bay and provide a fertile environment for the seed to flourish, and the harvesting of the crop. A prior glance at the hillside would lead one to believe that the foliage was all dead and everything of value had been removed and consumed. How interesting then to see that even what appeared dead and lifeless could actually provide growth and life to something.

Have you ever looked around (or in the mirror) and wondered if someone was spiritually dead? It appeared their years of planting seeds, maintenance and spiritual harvest may be past. Or do you feel your own days of spiritual investment in others is also part of your history rather than your future? I encourage you today to remember,

God is able to use anything and everyone. Just because something appears dead to others, doesn't mean God can't use it to bring life to someone else. Just as the cattle will feast upon the corn stalks and use them for nourishment, your journey and life challenges may be exactly what sustains someone else in a season where their own heart feels cold.

Don't be discouraged. There are seasons to life. There are times God may be calling you to be the seed planter and others when your job is to help people keep their lives free of weeds. Or are you in a season where you get to harvest. Perhaps someone else has done the planting, and you have the joy of bringing them to Jesus. ("I sent you to reap what you have not worked for. Others have done the hard work, and you have reaped the benefits of their labor. [John 4:38]") Are you feeling discouraged with your season? You want to be planting, weeding, or harvesting? Are you instead in a season where you're giving all you have left? The stalks that seemed to have given their all, God found further use for. ("For everything there is a season, and a time for every purpose under heaven: a time to be born, and a time to die; a time to plant, and a time to pluck up that which is planted; a time to kill, and a time to heal; a time to break down, and a time to build up; a time to weep, and a time to laugh; a time to mourn, and a time to dance; a time to cast away stones, and a time to gather stones together; a time to embrace, and a time to refrain from embracing; a time to seek, and a time to lose; a time to keep, and a time to cast away; a time to rend, and a time to sew; a time to keep silence, and a time to speak; a time to love, and a time to hate; a time for war, and a time for peace. [Ecclesiastes 3:1-8]") God isn't finished with you yet. Don't misinterpret your current season. Trust God in it. Embrace it. It may be the best season yet for you. It may be the hardest season yet for you. God's in charge. He knows what He's doing. Rest in the knowledge that even in seasons of death (like the stalks in the field), God can and will use you. And the beauty from it will be beautiful.

"To all who mourn in Israel, he will give a crown of beauty for ashes, a joyous blessing instead of mourning, festive praise instead of despair. In their righteousness, they will be like great oaks that the LORD has planted for his own glory. (Isaiah 61:13)"

THE HARVEST

If you've been driving down the backroads of Iowa lately, you have likely noticed the significant transformation taking place in the fields right now. Almost overnight it seems the bean fields have gone from a beautiful, luscious green to a lovely golden color. There's almost a sadness that settles into my heart as I see the season of life and growth coming to an end for another year. I love summer. The warm days, the freedom of tromping around barefoot, and the joy of seeing everyone outside in the evenings. However, anyone who has grown up on a farm or living in the agricultural communities of Iowa knows that this is when the harvest comes. All summer the crop has been growing. From the first seed planted to the hot, humid days of pollination, it all climaxes with the harvest. But in order to be harvested, death must come.

Where are you at in your journey today? Are you planting seeds in someone's life, or have they been planting in yours? Good, because while it may not yet be the season of harvest for them, there has to be a seed planted in order for the growth of their faith to happen. Are you helping to pollinate, or is someone helping you? Good, the quality of the ear could be determined by this investment into someone's life. Perhaps you have been called to cultivate? Help them take out the weeds. (Does anyone cultivate anymore?)

Regardless of your role, you can be part of the process leading up to the harvest. Or it could be your life that's about to reap the harvest.

Keep in mind, no farmer I know ever hops in their combine and goes out to harvest a crop that wasn't planted. The crop may have weathered dry seasons, wet seasons, or even hail and high winds. But what is left needs to be brought into the bins. And what is left will reap the reward. In farmers' lives it's financial, but in our spiritual lives it's much better. It's a closer relationship with Jesus. It's Him receiving more glory, and you receiving more love. It's others around you being touched by His love through you. Be patient. Regardless of your current season of life, the harvest will come. Embrace where you're at and don't try to rush through it. If God's planting something new in you or through you, give it time to germinate. Let it get watered. Let it have the warmth of the Son. Let it put down roots to weather the storms. And don't be afraid of the season where death takes place. Death is part of the harvest process. Until that death takes place, there cannot be a harvest of the fruit God has grown in you.

As you enjoy the crispness of Fall, let it be a reminder to you of God's great love. He's investing in you. He's investing in someone through you. Or, quite likely, He's doing both at the same time. Ask yourself today, where does He want to grow me? What has he planted fresh in my life? Am I allowing it to grow? Am I willing to be the farmer in someone else's life? Help them grow? Or let go and let someone else be the growth they need. The joy in the journey is knowing that in every single season, God is there, and He has a purpose.

Oh, and one more thing, don't forget that after the harvest the land may appear barren and cold. Empty almost. But the grain has been harvested, and it is being used to support and feed people through the cold months of winter. If you're in a season of living on your reserves, hold tight! Spring is just around the corner!

LITTLE BUG

This morning a tiny little bug landed on my arm. Instinct said, "Squish it!" But for whatever reason, I just looked at it. It was smaller than the tip of my pencil and had these delicate little wings. I mean, honestly, it was an awe-inspiring creation for the Lord to give it wings, a heart, and a purpose.

If God took the time to create such intricacies on a bug, imagine the beauty He sees in us. We are His children. He loved us so much He gave His Son for us because He wants to spend forever with us! Do you see your beauty? Your worth? He does!

Check out Deuteronomy 10. He is our praise. The Amplified version included glory. When we are who He created us to be, He is praised and glorified. But even more so, He IS praise. He IS glory. He is awesome. He is the Creator Who loves us just the way we are.

He's crazy in love for you! Embrace the Love!

OIL ON THE ROAD

I absolutely love living in the country. Summer is my favorite because of the wide-open space and ability to be outside and just enjoy the quiet. But winter has its own set of advantages. There's nothing like a good snowstorm to keep everyone hunkered in and feeling as if you're the only people in the world.

There is one thing that we experience in the country, which those in town or on a paved road don't. Dust. Oh, I know, you get dust, too. But I would be shocked if you get it the way we do. There have been times when I hung clothes on the line, and I think they end up dirtier when I bring them back in because the dust sticks to the wetness. I watch pick-ups go by and their dust trail is almost like a cloud of smoke wafting and hanging. And since I like sunshine, doors and windows are open when possible. Thus, what is outside comes inside.

There's a wonderful solution which we invest in each year. It's an expense those who live in town may not know even exists. We pay to have oil put on the road, which holds the dust to a minimum. I know, right? Pay to dump oil on a gravel road? Oh, it is well worth it! The vehicles which go by hit the oiled spot and dust just disappears. It's fantastic.

I was thinking about it today, and it struck me how very symbolic it is of Jesus. The world is full of sin. Even people who seem like "good" people are sinful. It sometimes seems like it is hanging everywhere like the dust in the air. But in His immense and vast love for us, God sent Jesus. Just like the oil covering the road, Jesus' death on the cross and resurrection on the third day covered us. We're no longer defined by sin. As a person repents for their sin, surrenders their life and receives the free gift of salvation, God looks at us, and He now sees Jesus. Covered. "In him we have redemption through his blood, the forgiveness of sins, in accordance with the riches of God's grace. (Ephesians 1:7)"

Will we still sin? Oh, how I wish I could say we won't. Sadly, we will. But we are no longer defined by our sin. It doesn't control us. The more we are filled with the love of Jesus and His Holy Spirit's leading, the less we will walk in the flesh. "But you are not controlled by your sinful nature. You are controlled by the Spirit if you have the Spirit of God living in you. (Romans 8:9)"

Rejoice today! He's given the gift of Jesus to you! Open the gift and enjoy it. He's got you covered!

THE FLOOR

After 25 years of bare feet, raising children, farmer boots, and the children (okay and sometimes parents) sneaking pets into the house, we knew it was time to replace the flooring in our kitchen and dining area. The love of the years was evident in some of the stains. The white was turning yellow, and some spots just couldn't be scrubbed out any longer. I do believe my all-time favorite was the farm dust collecting between the woodwork and the floor where even scraping with a knife didn't seem to make it disappear.

We did our due diligence (this means two stores rather than just one) in looking at different floorings and settled on one we both liked. It sat for a couple weeks stacked neatly in piles awaiting installation. I headed to visit my mom in Arizona, and the work began. (Trust me, it was good to be gone. You know when your husband texts that he was mumbling your name over and over while stuck under the shelf in the closet, that nothing productive would have been accomplished, other than a potential marital dispute, by your presence.) It was while I was in Arizona that it occurred to me I had not mopped the old floor before I left. I knew it had been decided that laying the new flooring on top of the old would be a much simpler process. I don't know all the details why other than something with the flooring under the linoleum. Not being very insightful about that type of thing, I trusted my husband's judgement. BUT (yes I said but) it hit me while down south that the floor was not clean. It was beginning to really "stir my pot" to think that we'd have this beautiful new floor that was on top of last week's spills and spots. I did what every good wife would do (especially after receiving the text referencing my name being mumbled), I sent a text of my own asking John to mop the floor. Lol! Oh, yes, you can imagine. NO RESPONSE. I am the persistent type and when he called later, I ASKED if he had mopped the floor. Well, now I'm just laughing away, because I know his top priority is not the old floor. In fact, I suspect I could probably read his mind. First, it would be something to the tune of "if she wanted the floor mopped, she should have done it before she left." The second thought might be, "It makes no logical sense to clean a floor no one is ever going to see again." I actually received the third anticipated response, "I guess you'll never know." Oooh, avoiding the question with a flippant response. Ugh!

Here's the deal. Why do I even care about the state of the old floor? No one will ever know. Yet I'll know. The longer I thought about it, the more it made me think of David when he became king. He inquired as to whether anyone was left from the house of Saul. He wanted to show them kindness for the sake of his beloved friend, Jonathan. He was told by the servant Ziba about Jonathan's son, Mephibosheth. He was crippled in both feet. He requested Mephibosheth to come to see him. I suspect that would be a bit unsettling (for Mephibosheth) considering his grandfather had tried to kill David. Do you know the account? I wonder if David did the last thing Mephibosheth anticipated? David restored all of Saul's land to Mephibosheth. Oh, wait, it gets better. Mephibosheth was then invited to eat at David's table like one of the family.

David didn't expect Mephibosheth to get his act together before he came to see him. No, he brought Mephibosheth to the table and

THEN restored him to a place of honor. The kitchen floor is a perfect example to me. I wanted to clean the old before I got the new. It's exactly the opposite of how God works. God's invitation is to come to Him and let Him restore us (aka clean us up). We get to eat at His table, become part of His family, and be cared for all the days of our lives. Why? Because of His immense love and because of Jesus. God's love for us is huge. It's so big that He sent His one and only Son to die in our place. He took our sin upon Himself and defeated its control on our lives. If you're sitting around thinking you have to "clean up" your act (aka the old floor) before you can become new, you are wrong! You are invited to come to the table and let the King of kings restore you. The life of love, joy, victory, and freedom He has planned for you is beyond anything you can imagine. Are you a son or daughter of the king, but you keep forgetting and thinking you need to "fix yourself up" before He can really love you? Or better yet, He has called you to something and in obedience, and you followed His lead. But once you found yourself knee deep in the assignment, you forgot that He wanted to empower you and charged ahead on your own? Take a deep breath. Trust He loves you. And come running back to the table. A lot can be resolved overeating with the King every day.

I know I might sound like a broken record sometimes, but I cannot emphasize enough the importance of spending time in the Word. You don't have to change your behavior to spend time with God. Trust me when I say, spending time with God will change your behavior. If you try to put the cart before the horse, all you're going to get is nowhere. Because if you can whip yourself together to be good enough for God, well then, you wouldn't really need God. I for one have decided it's much easier to do it His way. He loves me and WANTS me to come to Him. Oh, trust me, I still frequently park my cart in front of Flicka, but God's Spirit is gentle and kind. He likes to quietly whisper in my ear, "Daughter, I've got this if you'll just get out of my way." Let's do it, let's go eat with our precious

Savior and be restored. I for one have decided to enjoy our new floor and forget the old one is even under there. After all, he may have pulled it up and not even told me. I know just as my husband loves me and does what's best, God loves me even more. Are you ready? Let's go have supper with the King!

David's restoration of Mephibosheth is found in 2 Samuel chapter 9.

NOTES FROM JOHN

W e had a great laugh this morning. John put a note on the stove several months ago. The oven temperature gauge (or whatever it's called) hadn't been working, so the oven would only work if it was set at 350. He got it working, but he wanted to be sure we were VERY careful when we pushed the button so it didn't break again. I thought it was adorable and sweet and didn't take it down.

So, today I came back from the field with Abbie (how he did this I'll never know, because he was in the field the whole time I was, and I left him there) yet somehow, he managed to leave another note. Yep, there it was. A note above the thermostat. Abbie likes the house cooler than he does, and he wanted to be certain it was clear the thermostat was NOT to be touched. (Yes, of course, she got creative and used her nose.)

Deuteronomy 6:6 says we should write God's words on the posts of our house and the gates. You have to admit, these signs caught

our attention! Does God have my attention as much as John's notes? Am I in His Word on a daily basis? I want to hear Him speak. I want to know His thoughts. I want to know HIM. I want to know JESUS. I want to follow the Spirit. Here we sit with the very thoughts of God in our hands. Why not spend time hearing how He thinks and how much He loves us.? He wrote it all down for us in His Word. It's the greatest love letter ever written. Enjoy it! He's on our side!

"These commandments that I give you today are to be on your hearts. Impress them on your children. Talk about them when you sit at home and when you walk along the road, when you lie down and when you get up. Tie them as symbols on your hands and bind them on your foreheads. Write them on the doorframes of your houses and on your gates. (Deuteronomy 6:6-9)"

LAWN MOWER:
PART II

Last year as we neared the end of the mowing season, it became apparent that we may need to upgrade our lawn mower. So, as spring approached this year, John began doing his research. I wasn't surprised to come home one day and have him tell me a new mower would be arriving at the end of the week. Yay! This would be a tremendous blessing considering the size of the lawn and the assistance with Abbie mowing the cemetery.

You know the feeling when you get something new and can't wait to use it? You know, because your life is going to be better, easier, and things will run more smoothly. Umm, not always. You see, our wonderful new lawn mower was a zero turn. Have you ever tried one? Well, I had. Several years ago, we test drove a zero turn and after running into a tree while attempting to maneuver it, I thought I had made myself **very** clear that I had no intention of ever driving one again. No thank you, sir. I'll take a steering wheel, if you please.

We've now had our lawn mower for about three months. I spent the first two driving the old lawn mower around. John would hop on the new one (and it did look nice because he could get closer to the trees), and I'd putz on the smaller one. One day I decided I was being silly, so I headed out to the shed to give it a whirl. I didn't tell anyone, but apparently John heard me attempting to start it. (Who knew, push this lever, pull the throttle, push that down, pull the handles in and ignore the thing that looks like a brake, because apparently it is simply decor.) I did get it started. And it died. I got it started again, and by this time my husband had arrived on the scene. Yep, just in time to watch me heading, headlong towards the wall of his machine shed. He's yelling "stop," and I'm yelling, "I can't!" Once I managed to get the thing stopped, I hopped off and stomped out of the shed like any mature 51-year-old woman would. (No machine sheds were harmed in the making of this devotion.)

Well, that put a quick end to my decision and John's willingness to allow me to use the new lawn mower. Until about three weeks ago. Abbie had the old mower at the cemetery, and I needed to get after our yard. I had one option. John happened to still be home so I asked (very sweetly) if he would **teach** me **how** to run the lawn mower. He agreed (hesitantly) and only under the condition he got to drive it out of the machine shed for me. And I then had to practice in the wide-open space and drive very, very slowly. Sigh.

You know, those things tend to have a mind of their own. I started out trying to figure out which hand needs to go which way to turn, back up, etc. And today, after mowing with it for a handful of weeks, it's as if I've always known how. Guess how you do it? You don't think! You drive by instinct. If I stop and try to think about what to do with my arms, I end up going in circles at top speed. If I just let my body do what it knows it needs to, all goes fine.

As I was riding on the mower today, it struck me how very much like our spiritual life this new mower has been. How? We need to stop overthinking everything! There is a reason Scripture tells us in 2 Corinthians 10:5 to demolish arguments and every pretension that sets itself up against the knowledge of God and take captive every thought to make it obedient to Christ. Because when we start listening to the lies floating around and ignore the Truth of the Gospel, we're almost guaranteed a crash of some sort.

You know the kind I'm talking about, right? Remember the lady who looked at you funny at the grocery store? You went home certain she must be annoyed with you, or you decided maybe she was just a nasty person. When, in all reality, she was thinking about her doctor's appointment and didn't even see you. Or what about your boss who was short-tempered with you? You allowed a tone you were spoken in to convince you that you are unloved and unworthy. Yet maybe they just had an argument with their spouse and took it out on you. What about a mistake you really did make? You're a failure? Nope, you're imperfect and forgiven. Or the ultimate ones, the ones we tell ourselves. I'm not pretty enough. I'm not funny enough. Etc. Etc. As long as we let that negative garbage run around in our heads, we're setting ourselves up to be controlled by something other than the Truth.

How do we recognize it? How do you know Truth from lies? Well, just as I needed to run the lawn mower by instinct, we need to listen to the Holy Spirit. He will prompt us. As you fill yourself with the Word, He will bring it to your mind when needed. His fruit is love, joy, peace, patience, kindness, gentleness, goodness, faithfulness, and self-control. If what you're thinking about doesn't bear this fruit, you're quite likely dwelling on a lie. And lies have a way of stirring you into behaviors you don't really want to be demonstrating. The Truth is always, always found in Scripture. If it isn't in there, don't believe it about yourself. If the enemy tries to tell you you're a failure, remember you are a child of God. Not feeling loved? Well, Jesus loved you enough to die for you. Rejected? Oh, He's covered that, too. You're accepted and redeemed.

As you head about the rest of your day, remember, don't overthink the little things. "Finally, brothers and sisters, whatever is true, whatever is noble, whatever is right, whatever is pure, whatever is lovely, whatever is admirable--if anything is excellent or praiseworthy--think about such things. (Philippians 4:8)"

THE LEADER

"Be very strong; be careful to obey all that is written in the Book of the Law of Moses, without turning aside to the right or to the left. Do not associate with these nations that remain among you; do not invoke the names of their gods or swear by them. You must not serve them or bow down to them. But you are to hold fast to the Lord your God, as you have until now." Joshua 23:6-9

Yesterday this verse jumped off the page at me. Does that happen to you? I find that's one of the ways God speaks to me. If a verse leaps, I want to be ready to catch it and pull it in close.

It brought to mind the time years ago when John asked me to sit in the loader of the tractor. We were picking apples and wanted to get the ones at the top of the tree. (We all know the best ones are always at the top of the tree, right?) While standing on the ground looking up, it all sounded workable. (Did I mention I'm afraid of heights?) All I had to do was TRUST John not to hit the wrong lever. Uh, no! Because we all know if he hit the wrong lever I was going to land with a splat on the ground and quite likely be too injured to get up and say, "See, I told you so!" I crawled into the loader like a good wife. (Did I also mention this was EARLY in our marriage?) He carefully lifted the bucket, and there I was being held WAY UP in the air by a chunk of steel and being asked to trust him to keep me up there safely while picking apples. As you can assume, it didn't go well. I soon found myself hunched over in the bucket with my eyes fixed on John hanging on for dear life. He's in the cab chuckling away, finding the entire thing quite comical. I believe those were encouraging words he was sending my way over the motor of the tractor (let's face it when they're in the tractor it's all about the game of charades because you can't ever really hear what they're saying), but it was hard to tell as he was laughing. Well, laugh all you want, but I'm NOT letting go of the sides of the tractor, and I am NOT going to pick the apples up at the top of the tree. It's not that I didn't want to be helpful. No, it was fear. It was a lack of faith that the bucket would hold. It was looking at the distance from the top of the tree to the ground. (And let's just be honest, I'm not that good of a cook so if John had any secret thoughts of getting rid of me, it would have been a convenient time to do it and call it an accident.) I was no longer focusing on John's love to hold me up there, but I was instead focusing on the fears associated with what could go wrong. Ridiculous? Yes. Did it feel real at the time? Absolutely. (FYI: I screamed until he put me down. I asked for his recall of this story, and he tells me we never even got two feet off the ground the way I was carrying on in the loader. Mission: Incomplete. Husband versus wife perspective: Much different.)

I can't leave this story without sharing the same scenario last year. Our daughter came to the farm and the apples needed to be picked at the top of the tree. What a warrior! John had her in the loader of the bucket, put it right up into the branches of the tree, and she plucked away like no other. (The apples really ARE better at the top of the tree.) They are bigger, juicier, and much more plentiful up there! There was no screaming and no gripping the sides of the loader. (Of course, this is the same person who felt it would be fun to jump out of a plane for her birthday. However, that's another devotional.) Can you see the difference? She trusted her father not to drop her. She knew, no matter what, her dad was not going to let her get hurt. There was not a doubt in her mind that his love for her would not allow him to ask her to put herself in harm's way. (Now mind you, I was standing underneath the bucket, because I felt a backup plan was a good idea and was fully prepared to catch her if necessary.) As a result of her faith in his love, the blessing was greater. The apples were bigger, more plentiful, and even seemed less wormy. Trusting his love brought greater blessing!

It's no different with our heavenly Father. His love far exceeds that of an earthly father. He tells us He knows the plans He has for us and they are for good and not for evil. His love is deeper and wider than we can even imagine. If you were the only person on earth, Jesus would have still died on that cross for you. It's because of His death, we know He loves us. It's why I now include the word trust right alongside His commands to obey. The word *obey* used to bring to my mind a fear of punishment and oppression. We don't have to obey out of fear. Oh, no, we can obey because we trust Him. So when God commands us in Joshua to be strong and obey all that is written in the book of the Law and not turn to the right or to the left, we know obeying Him will be for our best. It will bring God glory and us joy.

I just can't leave without making the connection to the right and left. While in this context, I believe God is referring to a direction off the path of obedience, I couldn't help but make the connection with political lingo. We would be hard-pressed to flip on social media and not see a reference somewhere to the right or the left. I think it's why I found it so interesting. God told us not to turn right or left. He said, "Be strong and obey!" As our focus becomes obedience to the heart of God, we can step out in faith and trust His way is the best. He is asking us to trust Him. Personally, I've found that if I'm going to trust Him, I need to know not just what He's asking of me, but I also want to know Him. I want to know when He asks me to do something, I can crawl into the bucket and trust it isn't going to tip. I'm not going to fall. I can trust my Daddy. After all, He spoke the world into existence. He saved Daniel from a den full of lions. He knocked down the walls of Jericho. The list goes on and on. Truth be told, He has never once failed me. What begins as baby steps of faith, He will grow into a confident walk.

What is God asking you to do today? Where does He want you to obey and trust Him? Yes, He is asking you to be strong. He will provide that strength through His Holy Spirit. A walk of faith will require you to trust. It will require you to lean into His character and heart of love for you. You are correct, your life will not look like what the world tells you it should. The result will be a life of relationship with the Creator Who loves you beyond comprehension. He is simply asking you to trust and obey. Step into the fear, crawl into the bucket, and pluck away. A life walking with the Savior and doing it His way may not be the easy life, but it is the best life!

FAITH

There are two things I enjoy about vacuuming. I like hearing the clunk and rattle of things being sucked up off the carpet, and I love the lines left on the carpet when I'm finished. I've wondered before what is actually clunking up my hose. I mean, honestly, if I could see something large, I'd pick it up. (I know, if you've seen my car, you are questioning me right now, but it is true!) And I am super disappointed if I finish vacuuming and there are no lines. I want to be able to SEE that I've accomplished something when I'm done. No lines? Well, what was the point?

Is this how we approach our walk with the Lord? Do we want to see what He's doing? Do we anticipate hearing His voice? It certainly makes the relationship a lot more fun! What about those situations where you aren't hearing His voice right now? Do you have circumstances in your life where you can't see the vacuum marks? You've asked God repeatedly, but it doesn't seem like anything is changing? What do we do then? How do we respond when God seems silent?

Scripture tells us "we walk by faith, not by sight." 2 Corinthians 5:7 But how do we GET the faith? "So then faith *comes* by hearing, and hearing by the word of God. (Romans 10:17)" I can't emphasize enough the importance of being in the Word. As we walk out the ups and downs of life, it is Jesus Who will carry us through. Those times when your heart hurts so badly you think it might break in half. The times when you yearn to see someone you love know Jesus. Or the times when we are being asked to die to self so we can rise in Christ. Those times will come. I hate to be the bearer of bad news, but sadly we live in a fallen world, and pain and suffering are inevitable.

When they do come, let Him hold you. Don't pretend you have to be strong. It is when we are weak that we are strong. (And He has said to me, "My grace is sufficient for you, for power is perfected in weakness." Most gladly, therefore, I will rather boast about my weaknesses, so that the power of Christ may dwell in me. Therefore, I am well content with weaknesses, with insults, with distresses, with persecutions, with difficulties, for Christ's sake; for when I am weak, then I am strong. [2 Corinthians 12:9-11]") Because we surrender, and He shines.

Being in the Word in the up times will help with the down times. It is a tremendous reassurance to trust the heart of our Father. We know His heart by reading His Word. During the times in life when things don't make sense, those are the times we can say, "I don't know why, but I DO know Jesus." And Jesus is good. He is kind. He is loving. He will hold me up. Jesus will never leave me or forsake me. Jesus will empower you to walk through difficulties and even find joy.

I encourage you, don't let go of His hand. Don't be angry if you can't see the vacuum marks. God's always working for His glory and His best. He might just be vacuuming berber right now.

OOPS! WHERE'S
THE BAG?

I moved one of the chairs in the living room the other day and prior to putting it back, I wanted to vacuum underneath it. I got out the vacuum, zipped across the carpet, and then took the end off to suction up along the wall. It didn't seem to be working very well so I opened it up to check the bag. (See picture above.) Yes, it is exactly what it appears to be. I mean, really, it takes a very gifted person to accomplish a feat such as this! I had forgotten

to put a bag in last time I'd removed the old one and had been vacuuming away for who knows how long. I was surprised how much actually remained intact inside the vacuum. But removing the cover didn't do my carpet any favors. A quick trip to the linoleum found me using my hands to dump lots of "unknowns" into the garbage can. Gross!

I knew immediately there was a life lesson in this hot mess. How often in your spiritual life are you thinking everything is going well? You're going to the Lord, keeping with your quiet time, and attending church regularly? All is good. Right? Just to have an unexpected surprise like the vacuum! God starts to reveal a new area of sin in your heart He would like to deal with to give you more victory. Gulp. What? Because He loves us so much He will continue to reveal Himself to us until we reach heaven. Each day as we rest in and focus on His great love for us, we see ourselves more clearly. There seems to be so much sin that is rooted in our lack of trusting God and believing we are unconditionally loved. What is your go-to substitute for trusting you're loved? Food? Worry? Gossip? Overspending? Obsessively cleaning? (Trust me, that one isn't even on my radar!) Avoidance? Humor? Are you a workaholic? A complainer? You can fill in your own blanks. God will patiently wait until He knows we are ready to handle the revelation of an area He may want to evoke more freedom in our lives. We think all is going well, and He surprises us by revealing an area where there isn't a bag, and the guk of life is filling our canister. The Holy Spirit is our power source. He will expose and remove the sin and set us on the road to walk in even more freedom. He wants to take the sin which tries to distract and defeat us and toss it out. Or, better yet, use it to help free others. God promises if we confess our sin, He is faithful and just and will forgive us our sins and cleanse us from all unrighteousness. 1 John 1:9 It will not control you, but it does have to be surrendered. Oh, it may not be easy and an instantaneous deliverance may not be what you get. Sometimes, my friends, healing comes in the trenches. But you don't want it hidden away behind the door of your heart. Once exposed, it has no power over you. "This is the verdict: Light has come into the world, but people loved darkness instead of light because their deeds were evil. But whoever lives by the truth comes into the light, so that it may be seen plainly that what they have done has been done in the sight of God. (John 3:19-20)"

The Light is our Friend. He came in a manger born on Christmas, He lived a life of love and died on a cross, and He rose again after defeating the enemy. Don't let the fear of being discovered keep you in a place of bondage. And don't be afraid of any sin that tries to hold you. It has NO POWER over you. Jesus defeated you and set you free. If you find you've got an undiscovered mess today, don't hesitate to take it to Jesus in prayer. Share it with a believing friend who is willing to come alongside you and love you in it. Christians aren't out to judge. We're out to love each other with our imperfections. We're all on this journey together. You know the saying, "We're all just walking each other home." Rejoice today that God loves you enough to expose the dirt. Go to Him in prayer today and ask Him to begin dealing with it. His way. In His timing. In the arms of His love.

INSIDE JOKE

John and I have a joke between us. I love to rearrange the living room, paint, or do little household projects when he goes away for a few days. He has said he's almost hesitant to leave me home alone because he has this unease regarding what he might find when he returns. Well, last weekend he left on a golf outing for a few days, and I took full advantage of the time. I did a bit of rearranging with the furniture and hung a new picture on the wall.

I had a picture of the beach at Anna Maria blown up and knew just where I wanted to put it. Once I had it hung up, I noticed towards evening that the light came through the window, and it created a glare so you couldn't see the picture. I was disappointed so I decided to switch it out on a different wall. Since we had recently painted the living room, I didn't want to put nail holes in the wall above the TV, so I bought some command strips and put its replacement picture in place. They both looked great! I could live with this. I even chuckled a bit knowing John would not be so happy that I had not found the stud and placed it there. But I was looking forward to the teachable moment I would have when he came home, and I could demonstrate how studs and location were not always a necessity.

I'm enjoying my quiet evening when I not only hear but witness the command strip picture release from the wall, fall and hit the coffee table, knock over the TV, and send it toppling to the floor. Uh, oh! Breathe, Leslie. Breathe. I walk over, pick it up, and determine all appears to be fine. Until a couple hours later when I decided to watch TV. Nope. Not fine. We now need a new TV.

There are two morals in this story. The first, I was the one who needed the "teachable moment." The picture was heavy enough and should have (at the very least) had a nail. And second, John was right. (Yes, I just said that, Dear.) A heavy load needs to be secured.

This devotion was written during an unusual time. The fact that I had time to sit and write reflects it. I would have typically been in school enjoying the little people. However, there was a concern for the health and safety of the nation which caused people to implement social distancing, and schools were temporarily closed. It could have created an unease or anxiety. However, we are fortunate and blessed to have our lives secured in something much stronger than a stud in the wall. Our foundation and security are found in Jesus Christ. The Rock. All doubt about our eternity was removed by the cross and the empty tomb. Jesus took it upon Himself to carry our sins, allow them to be nailed through His hands and feet, and die a defeat through His death and resurrection. Sin no longer has power over us. He is willing to share His joy and peace even in the midst of the unknown. Because our eternity is known. The end of our story has already been written. We may not know what the middle looks like in detail, but we know the outcome. And we never journey through the details alone. Our Savior walks with us. He is in us. He loves us. And I pray He will be glorified through us.

Enjoy today. It is a blessing. Why? Because you'll never need to be six feet away from the One who loves you the most! "Don't you realize that your body is the temple of the Holy Spirit, who lives in you and was given to you by God? You do not belong to yourself. (1 Corinthians 6:19)"

WORKOUT

A couple weeks ago, I decided to try a new workout plan. It went really well for the first week. The second week (this week) I discovered perhaps my body wasn't quite ready for this intense workout. In fact, yesterday it even required a visit to the chiropractor to try and put everything back where it belongs. (Please tell me I'm not alone!)

I woke up this morning feeling much, much better than yesterday. Progress, because I was no longer feeling every single muscle in my chest, but also a bit defeated. Self-pity and striving were talking in my ear.

The story from John 21:6 came to mind. Remember when the disciples had fished all night and hadn't caught a thing? And Jesus showed up and told them to cast their nets off the right side of the boat? They caught so many fish they couldn't even haul them. Why was that? When Jesus is at the center of something, and He tells you to do it, you know it will work out for your good and His glory. (Keep in mind your good isn't always easy.)

Well, I had a pretty good feeling the Lord was reminding me to keep Him as my focus. Follow His way. Listen to Him. I have a tendency to let things like homework and workouts take precedence over devotions and Quiet Time with Jesus. Today, I can choose to be still and know that He is God! He will take care of the rest. Would you like to join us?

THE MOUSE

T he other morning, I was sitting at the kitchen counter when I was certain I heard toenails on our linoleum and saw a streak of movement across the kitchen floor. Okay. Just no. I don't and won't do MICE! After giving a big shout-out to my husband (who, praise the Lord, was still home), I crept very slowly around the island to investigate. I didn't see anything, and as much as I wanted to convince myself I had imagined the whole thing, I knew I hadn't. Where had the little critter gone? The only place to go was in the vent. Hmm...I confess relief that I couldn't find it but an unsettled feeling in the pit of my stomach. You know the one; knowing he was there but not certain where he was! Ugh.

I came home to find a trap set right below the kitchen sink and was told that there was one in the basement also. (Oh, did I mention my ornamental corn had been eaten when I got out my fall decorations? Of the three ears, apparently black is not the favorite color.) Well, I was fully supportive of the traps, and they offered a sense of ease to my spirit. It helped knowing if there was a critter in the house, steps were being taken to eradicate it. We've lived in this house for 24 years and have not once had a mouse. This is not a journey I am eager to embark upon should we have a war versus rodents on our hands.

Last night, I got a text from John with a picture of the critter. I say "the critter" fully aware there may be more than one! It sure felt good to know at least one little guy was no longer going to be scurrying around. This morning, I was sitting in the living room when I heard a "snap!" My heart stopped for just a moment until I heard John yell, "OUCH!" Guess who stepped in the mouse trap? Needless to say, it HURT!

Where am I going with all this? No, empathy isn't the goal. I challenge you to ponder something. After 24 years of no mice, I felt safe. It wasn't something I had to deal with. I could feel for the people who were dealing with it, but it wasn't my issue. Until yesterday! NOW it's my issue, too. Is there an area in your life where you felt safe? Where you didn't see the unexpected coming? The answer will be different for each one of us. Don't panic, God has and will fully equip you to deal with the challenge. His number one priority is your relationship with Him. Sometimes God will use those unexpected situations to draw you closer. He will expose a sin that you didn't even know was there. And just as the mouse had to die, there may be a part of you God is asking to die also. He says in John 12:24, "Truly, truly, I say to you, unless a grain of wheat falls into the earth and dies, it remains alone; but if it dies, it bears much fruit." Sometimes there needs to be a death in order for life to happen.

Perhaps you've been entertaining a "little" sin that doesn't even seem like a major thing. Maybe your situation was not a result of anything you did or didn't do, but through the process of dealing with it, God is going to use it to refine you and draw you closer to Himself. There may be some injuries in the cleaning out process (ask John's toe) but getting rid of what keeps us from the Lord will be well worth it in the end. "The thief comes only to steal and kill and destroy. I came that they may have life and have it abundantly." John 10:10 Trust Him on that one. If you are finding yourself in an unexpected situation today, don't be afraid to fight. God equips us to be armored up and stand firm. In the process of standing, don't hesitate to go through the death process and grieve the parts of yourself which have been dependent upon something other than the Father. He is our Source of all good things.

ZEKE AND THE HIDDEN FENCE

I was sitting at home one evening diligently working on my homework when I received a text from my husband. He had gone hunting down at my brother's. He said he had a surprise for me. I could tell by the text it was a good surprise! I couldn't wait to see what it was! Of course, like any good wife, my mind started to try and guess what it might be. My first thought was that he probably got a deer. (He would consider this a great surprise. It maybe wouldn't be quite as high on my list.) However, I realized if that were the case, he would be on his way home and not still at my brother's. I knew I'd just need to wait and see.

A few hours later when I heard John pull in, I got up and headed to the door. I hadn't built this up to be anything too stupendous, but I was a little fired up, nonetheless. As he walked through the door, there were no words to describe my surprise. I was speechless. Here he came with a grin from ear to ear escorting what looked like a full-grown dalmatian with a head of brown and black. I don't really know why I was so shocked. I like dogs. It just wasn't what I expected. I even jumped and screamed a bit when "Zeke" came to receive some new home love.

It turns out Zeke is not a dalmatian. He is a purebred English setter. (Free, I might add. One of God's blessings to our family.) His coat is a beautiful soft white with black spots. Now envision adding to this white with black polka-dotted body an intriguing brown and white face. He truly is a gift. (Just a side note: If you send your husband to have a playdate with your brother, you should anticipate "surprises" and be prepared for anything.) Once over the shock of owning multiple dogs, I've come to love Zeke and see him as a true gift to our home.

Hang with me, I'm going somewhere with this story. You know I like to lay the groundwork first. Well, Zeke is a hunting dog. He is beautiful to watch as his nose goes up in the air, and he sniffs everything around him. He is also a runner. He will tucker out our other dog within minutes because he seems born to explore. He just can't sit still. And he has discovered our neighbors have dogs, and he wants to be friends. Yep, this is a problem for the Gustafsons!

We are considering our options for Zeke. We want him to have the freedom to run around the yard but need to limit his excursions to the neighbor's house. We were looking at a couple of options and discussing which might work. There are underground fences which will give the animals a little shock to keep them from crossing the road. Or there are antennas we could put in the house which will give him so many yards around the property. We want him to have the freedom to run the farm, just not cross the road. The underground fence seems like a good idea to me. He could go anywhere but near the tree line. He would have the illusion of freedom. He could go anywhere he wanted to go except where he's not supposed to.

Wow! What does that remind you of in your spiritual life? Galatians 5:1 tells us, " It is for freedom that Christ has set us free. Stand firm, then, and do not let yourselves be burdened again by a yoke of slavery." You see, we can go to church and walk out our lives as a believer. We can love Jesus and desire to serve Him. But the question I have to present today is, is there more? Are you operating in the fullness of God's Spirit? The same God Who arrived at Pentecost in the book of Acts, "Suddenly a sound like a mighty rushing wind came from heaven and filled the whole house where they were sitting. They saw tongues like flames of fire that separated and came to rest on each of them. And they were all filled with the Holy Spirit... (Acts 2:2-3)" is the same God we serve today. The disciples loved Jesus. They followed Jesus. They worked side by side with Jesus. And when He returned to heaven, He sent His Helper, His Spirit to fill them with power. "...you will receive power when the Holy Spirit comes on you; and you will be my witnesses in Jerusalem, and in all Judea and Samaria, and to the ends of the earth. (Acts 1:8)" His Spirit is not gone. We are not left here without the Helper. And He has given us the same power and authority he gave to them.

Are you like the dog who has the illusion of freedom? (Don't get me wrong, the dog has some freedom.) Or is there more? Do you need to disconnect the hidden fence that is holding you back? Is there a lie you've been believing that has kept you from pressing in further to what God has for you? Has doubt been knocking at your door? Maybe you're just distracted by the things of life? (I know I found myself today going back to the Father apologizing for not being a better listener.) Am I the only one who sits down with Jesus and then remembers what I need to do...you can fill in the blank....and then hops up and leaves Him to throw in the load of laundry?" I just want to encourage you to hunger for more. Rest in His love while seeking as much of Him as you can get! Because, "You, dear children, are from God and have overcome them because the One Who is in you is greater than the one who is in the world. (1 John 4:4)"

WALK IN AUTHORITY

As you know from a previous devotional, we have acquired a couple of new dogs this year. We have Zeke, our English setter. We also have Buck, a labradoodle. Buck is pure black and the size of a small moose. He's a loveable pup (still not a year old) and likes to knock us over if he wants attention and isn't getting it. While a loveable dog, Buck is also territorial. He was groomed by our dog of many years who recently passed. Freckles taught Buck to walk the perimeter of our farm every day. I'd come home from work to find them both laying in the ditch "guarding" the farm from the neighbor dogs across the road.

The neighbors also have two dogs. I don't know the breeds of their animals, but one is what John refers to as an "ankle biter." (You can picture it, right? A small dog who likes to yip a lot.) The other day as we were in our yard raking, the neighbor dogs headed across the road to make their presence known. As you can assume, our dogs went on high alert. One neighbor dog remained on the road barking and barking. The little, tiny dog came prancing right on over into our yard. He was barking and barking and carrying on as if he were the size of a St. Bernard with the ferocity of a Doberman Pinscher. Yet in all reality, he is the size of a large rabbit.

John was calming our dogs, commanding them to stay. They did well for a while. Finally, they had enough. Zeke took off like a streak with Buck by his side. It didn't take long for the visiting dogs to head for home. Everyone made it home, safe and sound with no injuries.

As I thought about the situation, I could see the Lord all over it. How often do you start your day as Buck was taught? Do you circle your property and make sure all is safe? Do you start your day in the Word? Do you ask the Lord for His wisdom and guidance for the challenges and opportunities you will have that day to glorify Him? Do you take a check on anything in your life that may need to be addressed? Is there an area of vulnerability that may need to be taken to the throne?

The larger lesson from the visiting dogs was the reminder of our authority in Christ. How often does the enemy come to visit? He stands yipping and barking across your yard? He's in your head tossing out lies. He's taunting you. He loves to accuse you that you're not good enough, you're a failure, or get you all wrapped up in fear. All the while, you stand there with the authority of Christ the size of the small moose! Buck was obedient. He listened when John told him to stay. He was directed to ignore the little dog. It is a good lesson to always obey and trust the heart of God. Yet the time came when the yappy dog needed to go home. He was in Buck's yard and making a scene. It was not his home. It was not his property. He did not have the authority to be there. Buck and Zeke did. Buck did what we as believers need to do. We need to pick up our sword and engage in the battle. Take authority over the enemy. Don't even let him hang out in your yard. The enemy will spew nothing but lies. God has given you power and authority over the darkness. As His children, we need to step into that authority and walk in the victory He has given us. Own it. Walk in His power and grace. John 14:12 says, "Very truly I tell you, whoever believes in me will do the works I have been doing, and they will do even greater things than these, because I am going to the Father." (NIV) Luke 10:10, "Behold, I have given you authority to tread on serpents and scorpions, and over all the power of the enemy, and nothing shall hurt you." (ESV) James 4:7, "Submit yourselves therefore to God. Resist the devil, and he will flee from you." (ESV)

You do not have to tolerate the enemy's behavior in your life. You do have to walk in obedience to Jesus and God's Word. Remember, you are the big dog in the battle, because you are filled with the power of the Holy Spirit! The battle ended on Easter morning when Jesus walked out of that grave. If you have received Jesus Christ as your Lord and Savior, you are His child. "... to all who did receive him, who believed in his name, He gave the right to become children of God, who were born, not of blood nor of the will of the flesh nor of the will of man, but of God. (John 1:12-13)" Let's walk in our authority. Don't listen or tolerate the lies and constant yapping. Take the authority given to you in Christ and walk in victory. "...for everyone born of God overcomes the world. This is the victory that has overcome the world, even our faith. (1 John 5:4)"

"And he called the twelve together and gave them power and authority over all demons and to cure diseases. (Luke 9:1)"

"And these signs will accompany those who believe: in my name they will cast out demons; they will speak in new tongues; they will pick up serpents with their hands; and if they drink any deadly poison, it will not hurt them; they will lay their hands on the sick, and they will recover. (Mark 16:17-18)"

"Then Jesus came to them and said, "All authority in heaven and on earth has been given to me. (Matthew 28:18)"

PURGING
REGRETS

Have you ever had something you just loved, and it broke, or you gave it away? I used to have this funky top which was very boho before boho was a thing. I loved that top. I wore it several times and always felt excited when I put it on. However, as can happen, I decided maybe it just didn't fit "who I was" anymore. I struggled with the idea, but eventually put it in my pile to go to the consignment store. You will never guess what happened. I began to think about that top all the time! I regretted giving it up and wished I hadn't. You can just imagine what happened, can't you? The next time I was at the consignment store looking around, I noticed the top was still there. I told the salesclerk how much I loved it and regretted getting rid of it. She reminded me that the shirt was still mine, and I could take it home if I wanted. So, I did! You want to know the crazy thing once I brought the shirt home? I do not recall ever wearing it again. It just didn't fit the same as it used to. After a couple of years of sliding it back and forth in the closet, it went back to the consignment store, this time never to be seen again.

As I began to look at the book of Joshua, it didn't take long to notice that Moses was gone, and God had appointed and anointed Joshua to be the new leader of the Israelites. Check out Chapter 1:2.

What is God telling Joshua about Moses? He tells him that his servant is dead, and he needs to get ready to cross the Jordan River and head into the Promised Land. I don't know why, but that strikes me as really funny. Isn't it obvious that Moses is dead? We will come back to that in a moment, but if you have your Bible handy, open up and read the end of Deuteronomy. I feel like there is something very important we need to check out.

As you read Deuteronomy 34, is there anything that sticks out to you? A lot of times the parts of the Word that jump off the page are specific to you from the Holy Spirit. It doesn't mean you're right or wrong if no one else notices, it just means God is a personal God and has a message specifically geared to how you think and how the two of you engage.

Read verse 4 again. I used to feel very bummed out for Moses. He got to see the Promised Land but never physically entered it. Isn't it amazing, though, that God allowed him to see it? And as he was gazing out over it, God is sharing all the plans and specifics of the area He is going to grant to the descendents. Moses had fulfilled his calling. God had blessed him with a mother who protected him from the Egyptians who were killing all the Hebrew babies. He orchestrated the princess taking a bath at the exact time to find Moses in the river and then allowed him to be raised with the love and care of his mother and ultimately an education provided by the princess in the palace. All of those situations, along with lessons learned from his poor choices and learning to manage boundaries, had prepared him to lead the people out of bondage. They were free. Spiritually, we are free. Is there a pastor, counselor, or special friend somewhere who has helped lead you out of the bondage of spiritual death? Is there someone who loves you so much they have told you about our beloved Jesus? Guess what? Their job may have been to lead you to Jesus, but that doesn't mean your spiritual journey has ended. It has only just begun!

After Moses saw the Promised Land, what happened? He died. But THEN what happened? Isn't it absolutely amazing? God buried him. Did you catch that? Yes, GOD buried him. Personally, I find that incredible. Moses and God were such good friends that they sat on the mountain together before his death and looked out over the Promised Land. God was with Moses when he passed and then buried him. Did you notice in verse 6 where he was buried? No? Oh, why do you think no one knew exactly where the grave was? Hmm, is it possible that God didn't WANT anyone to know where the grave was? Perhaps God didn't want people to get stuck in the wilderness. What if they had known where the grave was located? Would they have decorated it each year to remember and honor Moses? Is Moses the one who would be glorified in those moments rather than God? God knew that Moses had fulfilled his role and wanted the people to prepare to move forward. He didn't WANT them to settle for freedom from Egypt but never enter the Promised Land. Can you see how that relates to our spiritual lives? God has freed us from an eternity of separation by sparing us from hell. He gave His one and only Son to die in your place. You are out of "Egypt," so to speak. You are free. BUT are you still wanting to hang on to the lifestyle of wilderness mentality? Are you so stuck in the religious thinking of how you've always done church that you haven't yet taken the steps necessary to reach the Promised Land of victory God has for you personally?

Check out what God allowed the people to do in verse 8. He allowed them time to grieve. It is so important when God calls you to a place of new to take the time to grieve what you are leaving behind.

Years ago, God began dealing with an anger issue in my life. I would fly off the handle at every little thing for no good reason. It was an unhealthy learned behavior. As God began to change my heart to one which responded to frustration in love, I also began to grieve. You see, anger and I had been friends for a long time. Regardless of what I had going on, I could count on anger to be there with me. Once I realized I didn't need anger any longer, because I had a God who wanted to fill me with joy, I had to say goodbye. Unhealthy anger did not get to be a part of my promised land. But I still had to say goodbye to this emotion which had become an everyday part of my life. Just because something isn't good for you doesn't mean you won't grieve it as you release it.

What have you had to grieve as you let go, or what do you still need to grieve and surrender?

Can you see how once God buries it for you, it might be in your best interest not to know where He puts it? There will be no going back to sit and remember the good ol' days when a good temper tantrum would jazz up the adrenals and get you going. Oh, no. After you grieve the loss, even if the temptation exists to go back, once God buries it in an unknown place, you won't be able to return even if you want to. The anger served its purpose in my life for a long time, but just like Moses' calling had ended so had the role of anger in my life. What might you be holding onto that God wants you to let Him have? Are you willing to let God have it and bury it so that you won't be able to return?

Now read Joshua chapter one. What is it again that God spoke to Joshua? God told him Moses was dead. Okay. Now then...... oh, that was a big "now then" God's saying, the old is gone and the new has come. Check out Isaiah 43:19 And aka Joshua, you are the new thing.

God comes to Joshua and gives him the directions to relay to the people. Moses had prayed for Joshua in Deuteronomy and mentored him into the role of leader. God specifically chose Joshua. Joshua had proven faithful when the spies were sent into the land.

God had groomed him for this role. Yet even Joshua needed God to say it to him very clearly, "Moses my servant is dead." Was God using this moment to remind Joshua that "you're it?" God began speaking to Joshua, and what did He tell him?

Yep, God said in Joshua 1:2 "...you and all these people, get ready to cross the Jordan River into the land I am about to give to them..." So, Joshua, get ready! Not only did God tell him to get ready, but He also told him what He was going to do once they got there. What did God promise Joshua? What is God promising you? What is He asking you to lead? Participate in? Follow Him into? Is He handing you something that you've been hesitant to step into? What's holding you back? Is it time to let go of the past, grieve what's been holding you down, and look ahead? Or better yet, look up? Is God telling you it's time to cross the Jordan into your Promised Land? Because I'm telling you, God did not deliver you out of an eternity of damnation to have you wandering around in the wilderness. Uh, uh. He has an entire Promised Land for you. He is waiting for you to step into it in faith.

God said He would give them every place where they set their foot, as He had promised Moses. Oooh, good spot to bring up Moses. No, God isn't saying, "Rats, I wish Moses was here." No, He is reminding Joshua that HE was with Moses, and HE would be with Joshua. It's good to take time to remember what God has done as He's leading you into something new. Why? Because the God Who was faithful before will be faithful again. Woo Hoo! Can you name five small things this past week in which God has faithfully provided? How about some major things during your lifetime? Was God faithful? Will He be faithful again? Luke 11:11 tells us that no father whose child asks for bread is going to give them a snake. We can bank on it when God tells us it's time to move that He fully intends to go with us. After all, Scripture tells us that God's Spirit lives in us (1 Corinthians 3:16) so we KNOW He will go with us.

Notice verse 4. What is God doing in this verse? He is laying out exactly where the Israelites' territory will be. And then check out verse 5-7. Oh, ya! "No one will be able to stand against you all the days of your life. I was with Moses, so I will be with you; I will never leave you nor forsake you. Be strong and courageous, because you will lead these people to inherit the land I swore to their forefathers to give them. Be strong and very courageous. "

What territory has God promised to you? He has promised you spiritual territory, that's for sure. His promises are all over the Word of God. Galatians 5:22-23 reminds us of the fruit that is ours because we have the Holy Spirit living inside of us. Friends, it is God's promise that we live in joy, peace, patience, kindness, goodness, gentleness, and self-control. It's part of our promised land. What other territory has He promised you? What about authority? Read Luke 10:19. You have the power to overcome the enemy. It's part of your promised land in Christ. The list goes on and as you get into the Word and read the Word, you'll discover more and more. Has He promised you a territory for ministry? If God has promised it, He will fulfill it. He is the same God who promised to never leave us or forsake us. He has not changed.

Are you living with a Promised Land mentality? Are you believing God? Do you know what the Word says about Him? Do you know what it says about you? Do you know you can live a life of victory over sin? Do you know you are loved unconditionally, and nothing will ever change that reality? Stop and pray. Ask God's Spirit to reveal to you whether you are living in the wilderness or the Promised Land. Is there anything specific He is bringing to mind that He wants you to allow Him to bury? Are you ready to step into the Promised Land He has promised you?

Well, get ready! We are about to travel with Joshua into the Promised Land. God isn't finished with His promise to Joshua, and we will pick it up again. The battles will still exist, and the Promised Land needs to be won, but the victory is promised. We know the end of the story. Take God's hand today and trust that whatever He is asking you to give up will be replaced by something soooo much better.

RIGHT, LEFT, OBEY

"Be very strong; be careful to obey all that is written in the Book of the Law of Moses, without turning aside to the right or to the left. Do not associate with these nations that remain among you; do not invoke the names of their gods or swear by them. You must not serve them or bow down to them. But you are to hold fast to the Lord your God, as you have until now." Joshua 23:6-9

If you have the opportunity to read through the book of Joshua, I'd strongly encourage it. God's Word is alive and active. As you read it, the Spirit will speak. Joshua 23 has part of the verse which reads, "...without turning to the right or the left." Do you have a social media account? You may just want to scroll through and see pictures of your friends and loved ones but find it difficult to avoid stumbling across those two words. Right and left. I think that's why they caught my attention. Apparently, God felt them important enough to use them, so let's see what He had to say. Isn't it interesting how He chose to include them in Scripture? He said to "be careful to obey all that is written in the Book of the Law of Moses, without turning to the right or to the left." Wow! He said **don't** go right and don't go left. Instead, He said, "...be careful to obey..." There's a word that doesn't pop on my social media account very often. Obedience. What does obedience require? Well, according to the first part of the verse it requires strength. God said, "...be very strong." Apparently, obedience takes strength.

The world currently provides lots of opportunities to turn right and left. There are gods and sin vying for your attention every time you turn around. They can become familiar to the point it is difficult to identify them. Oh, they don't jump up and down and holler, "Hey, I'm here to tempt you." No, they like to wrap themselves up in niceties to disguise their true intentions. The use of the word gods doesn't just mean statues erected as idols. It's anything you worship that absorbs your time, attention, and commitment over your relationship with Jesus. The pursuit of wealth can become a false god. Bitterness can become a false god. Self-pity can become a false god. Your personal appearance can become a false god. How much time do you spend on social media? Yep, it can become a time sucker as well. You can fill in your own blank. What about sin? Do you justify certain sins because you don't want to give it up? Do you like to take God's name in vain? Ouch. How about gossip? Do you engage in conversations that are actually harmful to others? Are you the idol? Do you value your ability to care for yourself above Christ's? Or are you walking hand in hand with the Savior on your journey of faith?

Obedience is not always an easy lifestyle. The longer you walk with the Lord, the more time you spend with Him, and the more you surrender to the leading of the Holy Spirit, the easier it can become to trust that His heart is for you. Obedience will stem out of your relationship with the Trinity. You will begin to recognize their voice and trust their call. Oh, it may have a cost. Obedience often does. However, the blessings far outweigh the loss. The safest and most joyous place to be is wherever the Spirit leads. He can be trusted. I encourage you today if or when you hear someone refer to the "right" or the "left," ask the Spirit to create a catch in your spirit.

Allow them to be trigger words for you that direct you back to the Word. God is very clear. Do not turn right or left. Instead, walk in obedience. "Enter through the narrow gate. For wide is the gate and broad is the road that leads to destruction, and many enter through it. But small is the gate and narrow the road that leads to life, and only a few find it. (Matthew 7:13-14)"

FIND YOUR LANE

The road to work has been under construction this summer. I appreciate that it had flaggers rather than the detour on gravel a couple years ago. The workers are now all gone, and the new road is smooth. It's a quick drive to and from work. As I was traveling the road the other day, I met a car. Typically, this would not even be a moment of registration to me. However, this day the Lord had something to say.

I realized as I passed the car, each of us going opposite directions, that there were no center lines on the road. However, it was not even a question that I would stay on my side of the road, and he/she would stay on theirs. No one hugged the middle, and no one was about to fall off the edge. We both knew that we had a "lane," and we stayed in it. Imagine if the body of Christ worked that way. God has blessed each of us with talents and gifts. Ephesians tells us "...that these are the gifts Christ gave to the church: the apostles, the prophets, the evangelists, and the pastors and teachers." Corinthians tells us more of the gifts, "Now to each one the manifestation of the Spirit is given for the common good. To one there is given through the Spirit a message of wisdom, to another a message of knowledge by means of the same Spirit, to another faith by the same Spirit, to another gifts of healing by that one Spirit, to another miraculous powers, to another prophecy, to another distinguishing between spirits, to another speaking in different kinds of tongues, and to still another the interpretation of tongues. All these are the work of one and the same Spirit, and he distributes them to each one, just as he determines. Just as a body, though one, has many parts, but all its many parts form one body, so it is with Christ. For we were all baptized by one Spirit so as to form one body—whether Jews or Gentiles, slave or free—and we were all given the one Spirit to drink." We've all been gifts of the Spirit. They are not for self-glorification. They are used to build the body of Christ.

Does your church identify the gifts of the Spirit in people? Does it encourage them to operate in their gift? Does it allow for people to share their gift to build the kingdom? Does it notice when a gift is hurting?

Can you think of times that perhaps your wrist was hurt, and eating was difficult? Maybe you had to adapt and eat with your other hand. What about times your knee has been sore? Have you had to walk differently? It is imperative that if the body is going to operate at its maximum potential not only do we begin to recognize and encourage the gifts of our fellow believers, but that we identify which gifts may be hidden because they are hurting. Does the gift of healing need to come alongside another believer to assist in restoring a broken heart or discouraged spirit? Do you know someone who was operating freely in their gifts only to experience a word of criticism and ended up bruised in the exchange? Part of operating in the gifts of the Spirit will involve the restoration of the hurting and the identification of people's strengths. Instead of allowing jealousy and envy to steal someone's gifts, we want to encourage, uplift, and demonstrate grace. We need to identify the lane God wants us driving in and not cross the centerline and crash our fellow believers into an accident. The Spirit will empower each of us in order to achieve His goals and build up His body. Let's take the time to ask

Him what He has for us and do our best to surrender to His will. And perhaps we need to also take a moment and reflect with Him as to where we may be trying to drive in someone else's lane. It could cause an accident if we are. It could get someone hurt. We don't want to guilt others into serving where they aren't equipped. We want to build the body to hear from the Father where He wants them to serve. We can encourage others but not push.

As you seek where to serve this week, ask the Lord where your lane is? What has He instilled in you to love? What are you passionate about? Do you see a need that you have the skills to address? God has given you gifts. Seek Him where to use them. And don't be afraid to encourage others to use the gifts you see rise up in them. We're all driving to the same destination; we may just be traveling in different lanes.

LET YOUR
LIGHT SHINE

Yesterday I was working on glittering the giant letters S-H-I-N-E to use on the parade float Saturday. As I was sprinkling away, I commented that it was getting to be a bit of a mess. My associate said, "I can't believe I just heard you say that! You love glitter." My response was, "Yes, but sometimes letting your light shine gets messy!"

Isn't there truth in that statement? Oh, I didn't say it to be profound. I was speaking literally when it came out of my mouth. (It was on the carpet, in my hair, all over the table, in the hallway….) But God's Spirit does what He does in my brain and I'm grateful He speaks in ways I can understand. It's true. Letting our light shine can be messy. And sometimes we forget it.

You see, life with Jesus isn't always easy. Oh, it's ALWAYS, ALWAYS worth it. Jesus is amazing. He's eventful. He brings a love and joy and peace that is indefinable. But, easy? Ah, no. I do believe there are certain aspects we make too difficult. We stress. We fret. We try to anticipate and figure it all out. That is just wasted energy. It's not living in faith that God is in complete control. He has things all worked out, and we can trust that. Things that sometimes appear bad can ultimately be used for good. But if you think about the life of Jesus, well they killed Him. A man who never sinned. He was perfect love. And he was killed because He didn't follow the "rules and expectations" of those around Him. Yes, I know He let them do it because He loves us and made that sacrifice to take away our sins. But I'd call that a bit messy.

It can be messy for us. I know I've said before that relationships are messy. I think it's fair to add to that statement that choices can be messy, too. Do I do this? Or that? Do I tell the full truth at the risk of losing a relationship with someone if they become offended when I am honest? Do you give up something you really love doing for something you know Jesus is asking you to do? What about guilt? Do you ever toss it into a conversation like salad dressing? You may not even know you're doing it, but are there guilt messages in what you say? Do you try unknowingly to use it as a form of manipulation to accomplish your goal? Will you give people the freedom they need to follow Christ apart from your expectations and opinions?

Or everyone's all-time favorite. Have you forgiven? Are you carrying around a grudge that God is calling you to let go of? Is it weighing you down? Is it feeling like letting it go will make things a bit "messy" for you? You have every reason to be upset. Angry. After all, if only you knew what they'd done. You'd be mad, too. Maybe. But carrying around all that anger and hurt is continuing to give the other person control of your life. It's not hurting them. It's only hurting you. Forgive.

Let go of it. It will set you free. Forgiving doesn't mean the hurt has healed yet. The pain may exist for a while. Remember, shining for Jesus can be messy. But trusting Him and doing life His way, well, it makes your light shine. People will see Jesus in you. The mess will be worth the shine. And, get this, it spreads everywhere. As Jesus has more and more of you, He will leave a little bit of the glitter and sparkle everywhere you go. It's Him shining. Praise Jesus.

"Let your light shine. (Matthew 5:16)"

THE GATE

I watched the most interesting event transpire today. A child had hit his chin on a piece of playground equipment and was experiencing tears. Of course, I picked him up to console him. I heard a very typical and standard response, "I want my mommy."

I usually respond in situations like this by saying, "I understand. Sometimes, I just want my mommy, too!"

After a few minutes of consoling, the child determined they wanted to go home. They headed over to the gate and stood holding onto the fence repeating, "I want my mommy. Mommy, where are you?" It was heartbreaking to watch. I asked another child if she would go and invite the child with the wounded spirit to play. Oh, my gracious! It was quite enjoyable to watch! She walked over, assessed the situation, and then without saying a word, she proceeded to open the gate!

I said, "What are you doing? Please don't open the gate."

Her response was priceless, "Well, he wants his mommy. So, I'm letting him out!"

There were several things that struck me about this situation. First, the child who had bumped their chin was clearly in pain. Oh, not physical pain. The bump had subsided quite some time ago. No, this was compounded with other needs. He had a pain that was making this particular injury seem far more extreme than it actually was. The other unusual thing was that, typically, the children on the playground are incredibly observant and will come alongside a hurting child. Today everyone seemed very busy. No one was responding. Perhaps the pain had gone on too long for them, perhaps they were preoccupied by their own needs or interests, or maybe they just didn't care? Until the child who went to help. The little girl who did was willing to set him free from the fence that held him enclosed. The thing she could see standing between him and the mother he was desperately wanting. She knew all she had to do was open the gate. Let him out. Give him what he wanted in order to pursue his freedom.

My question to you today is which person are you in this scenario? Are you hurting? Do you feel as if no one is watching? Is the pain valid? Or are you angry and crying about something that isn't the real issue? Is there a deeper issue which needs to be addressed? Are you the friend currently ignoring someone in their pain? Have you taken the time to come alongside and see if you can help? Often it is only connecting in the pain that is needed. You don't need to fix it for someone, just walk beside them. Or are you the young lady who is prepared to set them free? Are you willing/wanting to open the gate for someone? Can you show them what is holding them in captivity? Are you willing to assist in opening it so they can pursue their freedom in Christ?

None of these roles are right or wrong. It all depends upon where you're at in your spiritual journey. In fact, you could actually be all of the above. If you're hurting today, Jesus has a ready ear and is wanting to listen. Surrender your pain and fears to Him. He will take them and turn them into something of value. He promises to use all things for His glory when we love Him. He will comfort, uphold, and walk with you. Are you in a position to be a Barnabas? Can you walk alongside someone and offer them encouragement? See them. Offer comfort. Listen to their hurt. Connect with them in their pain. It may not feel like enough, but the love of Jesus is healing and miraculous. Or are you the gatekeeper? Is your role to open the gate and help someone walk to freedom? One role not discussed was that of the overseer of the playground. The one who could see an open gate was not the solution just yet. Because an open gate at that moment would not lead to the mother. It could have led to more problems. Trust God's timing. If you're seeking an open gate, and it hasn't yet come to fruition, perhaps God is asking you to wait just a little longer. It may not be you who isn't ready for freedom, it may be He sees the bigger picture and is putting everyone else in place. Your freedom may be what He is going to use to help free others in the process.

See where God wants to use you today. Are you ready? Are you willing? Can you surrender your pain? Will you walk alongside someone else as they journey through their hard season? And most of all, when the gate opens and freedom is yours, are you prepared to walk through it? God's waiting, and you won't need to journey through the gate to freedom alone. He will personally escort you into victory. Blessings.

"So if the Son sets you free, you will be free indeed. (John 8:36)"

CLEAN WINDOWS

I was having a great chat with my mom this morning. I asked what was on her agenda for the day, and she replied that she needed to wash her windows. She giggled and said, "I haven't done them since the spring of 2018." I had to join her in that moment of laughter, because if you were raised by her, you are well aware that is not a typical behavior. She went on to say that you really only notice the dirty windows in the morning when the sun hits them. "I don't know why I don't do them more often, because they look so nice when you can see clearly through them. But it's easier to just pull the shade."

Yep, when the Son shines on us, it does expose our areas of great need for Him. We were dirty. We were covered in sin. But when Jesus died on the cross, He washed us clean. As He takes up residence inside the heart of a believer, things become so much clearer. We see everything through His eyes versus through the eyes of the world. While it's not hard to surrender your life to Christ, it can feel that way at times. People think they'll have to give up so much. But walking with Jesus isn't about what you give up, it's about the amazing gift you'll receive. The areas of sin that seem more than you want to let go, I assure you what Jesus has to offer is much, much better. Sins we think are providing us with fun are really just weighing us down and keeping us in bondage. Freedom is ours. All we need to do is ask. Yet to all who did receive him, to those who believed in his name, he gave the right to become children of God. (John 1:12) I encourage you today, receive the gift. It might seem easier to just pull the shade, but in the process, it's blocking your view.

"Cleanse me with hyssop, and I will be clean; wash me, and I will be whiter than snow. (Psalm 51:7)"

TOWER OF BABEL

"But the Lord came down to see the city and the tower the people were building." Genesis 11:5

"Come, let us go down and confuse their language so they will not understand each other." Genesis 11:7

We were learning about the Tower of Babel in preschool this week. After reading it in the Children's Bible, I had some questions and went to look them up in the adult Bible. A couple of things in particular stuck out to me, and I thought I'd share them.

First, I thought it was interesting that the Lord came down to see the city and the tower that the people were building. (vs. 5) I always imagine Him right beside us (which He is), but it appears these people were not including Him in the equation. Were they needing a visit because He hadn't been invited to their planning party? Aren't you so thankful God does that for us? How often have you come up with a great plan or idea that you think is fantastic? Or maybe it isn't all that fantastic but seems like a great way to handle something. The people building the tower were being proactive and not wanting to be scattered all over the earth and thought this was their solution. But was their solution really an attempt to surrender to God's ultimate plan? Or was it an attempt to have their own way? Even though they didn't want to be scattered all over the earth, they were attempting to accomplish that feat by building a huge tower that would bring glory to themselves. Uh oh. Seems like maybe self was the focus of the motivation? Not God.

The other thing that jumped off the page was God referring to "Us" in verse seven. He was in constant relationship with the Son and the Holy Spirit. Relationships are so important to the Father that He's willing to come check out "what's going on in the city" and see what we're doing. Because God does not want anything to come between **our** relationship with **Him**. We are that important to Him. YOU are that important to Him. I am beyond grateful for a God with such an intense love for me.

Are you seeing how the two of these verses can tie together? Where in your life might you be working on "building a tower?" Are you pursuing something in which you forgot to include the Father? From the outside, it might even appear to be a great thing. But what are the internal motives? I have no idea what it might be in your world, but it's worth asking yourself the question. I know I was thinking of making a commitment to something recently, and my husband asked me to reconsider it. He shared his reasons why, and he was correct. It seemed like it would have been a great thing. It was even a "Jesus" thing. But what looked like a Jesus thing on the outside would not have been drawing me into a closer relationship with Him on the inside. And Jesus is concerned about our inside. He wants the real deal. He wants you with a passion and an intensity that are difficult to comprehend. So invite Him to come in and check out your city today. Invite Him prior to starting the building of your tower. His way is ALWAYS going to be the best way. He's way more concerned about you than you are about yourself. Trust Him. Trust His love!

ARMOR UP

The other day as I was sitting on the deck, I watched our dog Freckles go from a completely relaxed position lounging under the shade tree to full alert. He is getting older, so he doesn't take on that pose for no reason anymore. I watched him as he arched his back, hair stood on end, and a low growl came from his throat. Of course, by this time I'm wondering if I need to be concerned. I didn't see anything, but it was evident he did. I tried to see where he was looking and couldn't spot anything. However, we had seen a coyote run by the shed a couple days prior. Freckles remained where he was, ready for a fight if need be, but otherwise he didn't move. He didn't stand there very long when he decided the danger was past and laid back down completely relaxed again.

I was actually quite amazed. He saw the danger, was prepared to fight if necessary to protect his family and stood firm. He didn't chase the danger. He remained right where he was waiting to see.

Ephesians 6:10-18 talks about our need to put on the full armor of God so that we can stand against the devil's schemes. I think back to how many times I've responded to perceived threats like the young Freckles would have. I'd get in a panic and lose focus on what I was supposed to be doing. However, the mature Freckles was on

242

high alert and stood his ground. He didn't need to engage in battle in that situation, so he didn't. We can rest in peace knowing that it's important to be aware of danger, and God will most definitely show us when to be on alert. However, unless there is a need to fight, we can stay our course. Remain intentional about what God has called us to do. Rest in the shade of the tree in peace.

"Finally, be strong in the Lord and in his mighty power. Put on the full armor of God, so that you can take your stand against the devil's schemes. For our struggle is not against flesh and blood, but against the rulers, against the authorities, against the powers of this dark world and against the spiritual forces of evil in the heavenly realms. Therefore, put on the full armor of God, so that when the day of evil comes, you may be able to stand your ground, and after you have done everything, to stand. Stand firm then, with the belt of truth buckled around your waist, with the breastplate of righteousness in place, and with your feet fitted with the readiness that comes from the gospel of peace. In addition to all this, take up the shield of faith, with which you can extinguish all the flaming arrows of the evil one. Take the helmet of salvation and the sword of the Spirit, which is the word of God. And pray in the Spirit on all occasions with all kinds of prayers and requests. With this in mind, be alert and always keep on praying for all the Lord's people."

ANSWER HIS CALL

John invited me to ride along to pay a bill today (not my favorite outing), but then we got to stop at the local farmer's market. (FYI supper was amazing!) On the way our phones started dinging. It was rather interesting, because we were both in the same group text, but my phone would ring, and then his would follow or vice versa. Sometimes we would read them right away, and other times we'd ignore them. After a while, we both finally turned our phones on silent. We just got a bit weary of the dinging. (I turned mine off sooner, so his would ding, and since he was driving and didn't check it right away, it would ding again. He kept thinking he was getting new texts, because mine wasn't going off. But nope, just the reminder to check his phone. Ding. Ding. Ding!)

How often does the Holy Spirit prompt you to do something just like the message notification on your cell phone? Only, He doesn't often call on the phone and say "ding." He might place the thought in your mind to call a friend. Or maybe you saw someone with a flat tire, and He prompted you to assist. (I didn't say you had to change it for them.) Or even send an email or a card letting someone know you're thinking of them. There have even been times He's prompted me to pick up something at the grocery store.

How do you respond when He does it? Do you grab at obedience like we tend to with our cell phone? Do we hurry to see what it is He wants us to do and rush right into being prompt with following His lead? Or do we keep doing what we're doing and figure we'll get to it later when it's convenient? I hate to even ask, but do we ever hit the mute button and not listen at all?

I don't know about you, and I hate to admit it, but I suspect I've had times of each. But I know I want to be like David. I want to be a woman after God's own heart. I want to hear the still small voice (1 Kings 19) of the Lord speak to me and trust His love so much I obey the first time. John 10:27a says, "My sheep hear my voice, and I know them, and they follow me." I'd encourage you to be still and listen. Hear His voice. If you're struggling to hear Him, ask Him to help you identify when He's speaking. He's not trying to hide from you. He wants a relationship with you. He wants to talk to you. He loves you! Answer the Spirit's call. He's well worth listening to!

ROAD TRIP WITH MOM

I was heading out of town today and took a detour to pick up my mother to ride along. It occurred to me that by the time I went out of my way to get her I could have been halfway to my destination. However, I would have missed the very best part of the day! Hanging out with my mom.

Has it ever occurred to you that we sometimes have this plan of what our life is going to look like? We know where we're headed and suddenly life feels like it sends us on a detour. Maybe, just maybe, your detour is actually God's plan, because going His way holds the best part of the journey.

And, full disclosure, I volunteered to meet her at her house! I enjoyed the tour of her flowers while there!

Proverbs 16:9 and Isaiah 12:2. Check 'em out!

JURY DUTY

About a month ago, I received that little card in the mail labeled "Jury Duty." I confess my initial reaction was not one of enthusiasm. "Ugh! I don't have time for this" was my first thought. However, we live in an amazing country where we have the opportunity for a fair trial of our peers if accused of wrongdoing. I also know, if we want our country to walk with God, we need to be willing to serve in areas that might make us uncomfortable and engage in our judicial process.

I had no idea what to expect, because I'd never been called to jury duty before. It turned out to be quite a fun, social morning considering I knew lots of the other people there! Social distancing and masks can't hold down women who haven't seen each other in weeks/years. (See, already the blessings were beginning!) The jury selection process was not taking place at the courthouse to allow for more space to spread out. Thus, after sitting in the hall for a while, we were called into the church sanctuary.

A man on one side of the room who was wearing a suit and tie introduced himself as the judge. He appeared to have a kind and gentle spirit. He explained the process of jury selection while injecting humor to ease the angst of waiting. (I can certainly understand it's not super convenient to meet at the church versus the courthouse.) After watching a jury video and patiently waiting for things to begin, something very interesting happened. The judge put on his robe. I sat watching (I can't say anyone else was paying attention to this simple act) and was amazed at my own reaction. Something happened when the judge was all robed-up and sitting at the table. He became the person with the authority to run the room. (In all fairness, he had the authority the entire time. But my demeanor towards him changed.) He wasn't just a friendly guy in a suit giving us directions. He was in charge. He had authority. He had the full attention of everyone in the room. And he brought to light a side of God we hear about but perhaps don't get to see with such clarity.

If you're like me, you may have grown up with a mental picture of God as a judge created through the lens of personal experiences. As a kid, I had this feeling He was sitting and waiting for me to be naughty. I knew once that happened, I was going to "get it and get it good." It became very important to behave in order to maintain his love and acceptance. God graciously changed this misperception years ago. I no longer view Him as a mean and judgmental figure waiting to issue punishment should I make a mistake. (Let's face it, it is very difficult to behave all the time. Just the process of thinking can get me in trouble!) I now know God is kind, gracious, and loving. He is my advocate. He's for me. He loves me so much He sent His one and only Son to die in my place. (John 3:16) He's not sitting on a chair in heaven waiting to throw down the gavel when my mind wanders to how someone's shoes don't really match their outfit, or I get all irritated when a car pulls out in front of me when there's a mile-long stretch behind me free of transportation. (You know I'm not alone here!)

Here's the thing though. The judge was kind AND just. He had a responsibility to maintain order and deliver the sentence. It didn't change the fact that he was kind. He was just kind and just at the same time. These two things were aspects of his character that weren't separate from each other. They were both who he was. It was as if a light bulb went on in my head. This is how God is too! He is kind and loving. He has a great sense of humor and loves to teach us new things. He is forever our advocate and loves us unconditionally. He is never the guy sitting around in a robe waiting to "get us." No, He definitely is a Spirit of love. "For God did not send his Son into the world to condemn the world, but to save the world through him. (John 3:17)" The thing is, God is ALSO just.

The amazing thing about God as the judge is Jesus. You see, on that final day, we will stand before God. He will issue a judgment for our eternity. "Righteousness and justice are the foundation of your throne; steadfast love and faithfulness go before you. (Psalm 89:14)" And He will "read" the verdict. (Just a side note here, I didn't get chosen to be in the final twelve on the jury and therefore wasn't part of hearing a verdict read.) There is a consequence for sin, and in His justness, God will determine whether we will spend eternity separated from Him or in relationship with Him. But guess what? We can already know what our verdict will be. God is very clear in Scripture that "... to all who did receive him, to those who believed in his name, he gave the right to become children of God. (John 1:12)" God has already declared my sentence. He has spoken with His voice of authority and pronounced me "not guilty." I already know it! You can know it, too! The gift of Jesus is for everyone. As God looks at me, He sees me covered with the blood of Jesus. As a result, He issues a sentence of "not guilty." No, not because I didn't commit the sin, but because Jesus already paid my sentence. As He hung on that cross, He had my sin and yours upon Him. He defeated its hold on us and took it to the grave. He arose on Easter morning. The power of sin is defeated. As God looks at me, He sees Jesus' stamp of "sentence paid in full!" The verdict was determined. It is in and through Jesus we receive "Not Guilty!"

The gift of salvation is available for all of us. It's not just for a special few. It's not just for those who can control their thought life (this improves with the fullness of the Holy Spirit), it's not just for those who serve on church boards, and it's not just for those who never swear. It's for everyone. He died for every single one of us. The gift is available and waiting. It's yours for the taking. All you need to do is receive it. Not only will it change your life today by filling you with gratitude, hope, and peace which comes from forgiveness, but it will determine the final verdict. Our gracious and loving Father will look at us one day, see the blood of His Son covering us, and declare us "not guilty." I long to hear those words, "Well done, good and faithful servant! You have been faithful with a few things; I will put you in charge of many things. Come and share your master's happiness! (Matthew 25:12)"

What an incredible gift we've been given! If you haven't accepted this free gift awaiting you, please know all you have to do is receive it. God is waiting with His arms open wide. He loves you like crazy. He gave His Son who took our sin and condemnation upon Him. He's not waiting to condemn you for your mistakes. He has forgiven you. Will you accept His forgiveness? Will you embrace His gift? Will you surrender to a life filled with love and joy? A life lived in victory? God is right beside you. He yearns to hear that conversation. It can be short. It can be as simple as "Dad, I'm sorry. Thank you for the gift of Jesus. Please take my life and fill it with You. I choose to follow."

HIDDEN ROCK

Today, I was out mowing and didn't see the rocks hidden under the vine. (In all fairness, the vine was very lovely and full.). It made quite a clank! Did I mention it was a BIG rock, and I thought, uh oh, now John's going to need to sharpen the blades on the lawn mower, and he's not going to be happy about it! (I really didn't see the rock). But as I continued mowing and all worked fine, it made me think about two verses. The first being in Proverbs. As iron sharpens iron so one man sharpens another. And the second being from Hebrews. The Word of God is alive and active sharper than any two-edged sword.

What came to my mind was, am I keeping my sword sharp? The Word is always sharp, so I want to be in it and reading it. I don't want to become dull by being complacent about keeping my sharp sword ready. And, to top it off, I want to be the friend who can sharpen others with the Word. Sharing Jesus when needed! Praise God for His written Word!

THE BUSH

There is a bush I love. It is large and full. However, I've noticed lately that it has yellow leaves from lack of good nutrition in the soil. We have the same type of bush to the west of our house, and the leaves are just as green as can be. However, even though the soil lacks the nourishment to create deep colors, the yellow leaves actually offset the bush and make it really pretty. And the flowers are lovely.

Sometimes you may find yourself planted in an area where you don't feel like it's good soil. Maybe it's not an encouraging work environment, a difficult neighbor, or a down time in an important relationship. The list could go on. However, God will meet us and use us where we're at. Just like the bush, you can be beautiful right where He has planted you. Rest in the assurance that He is able. And it will be obvious it's His joy in you when you continue to thrive and shine by focusing on His Love and His grace! "The joy of the Lord will be your strength! (Psalm 28:7)"

THE GIFT THAT KEEPS GIVING

I have enjoyed the view out my kitchen window all summer. One of my students came walking down the hall with the beautiful yellow plant for Teacher Appreciation Day, and it set the tone for our entire color scheme of flowers. We knew we would be gone a couple times this summer so I put more of my annuals on the deck so watering would be easier for whomever came to do it. But I love looking out as I'm doing dishes and enjoying the yellow, blue, the red. It's gorgeous. All because a child shared the love of Jesus with me. Just think about that one simple, kind gesture you can make in someone's life. A stop to visit when everyone is outside in the evening, holding a door, sharing your flowers, mowing a lawn. You have no idea how it may set the tone for their entire day or summer or life. The gift that little girl gave me was a reflection of Someone bigger. It spreads joy. It makes me smile. Are we willing to share His love, or do we hide it? Are we willing to be open and honest about WHY we're doing it if we're asked? Do people know you love Jesus? Your large or small act of kindness could be the difference between a good day or a bad day for someone. Or it could be the difference between eternity with Christ or not. Wow. It's a bit sobering to consider it in those terms, isn't it? (Matthew 5:15-16) Neither do people light a lamp and put it under a bowl. Instead, they put it on its stand, and it gives light to everyone in the house. In the same way, let your light shine before others, that they may see your good deeds and glorify your Father in heaven. Plant the seeds of His love. Shine your light before others. God will be glorified through the grace you share.

IT'S FREE

The class and I were sitting at the rug getting ready for Jesus Time. The children were all eagerly anticipating what we were going to do. They could see I had a box full of coins. Oh, yes, they knew something good had to be in the works. I walked around the circle and gave each student a coin. They were all pretty fired up with this new development. I asked them if they knew what it was. Yes, money. Do you know what you do with money? Ninety-nine percent said, "Buy things with it." One child said, "Save it."

Next, I got out an even MORE interesting box. It was full of those oh-so-treasured trinkets. The ones that are great to a child and as an adult you hold your breath and pray they hold together long enough to make it all the way home in one piece. I made an offer to everyone. They could trade their coin for a toy, OR they could keep the money and get no toy. I went around the circle and asked each child. Again, all but one chose to buy the toy. One student kept the money. After everyone had their turn, I asked the question, "How much did your toy cost you?" One coin. I looked at the child who kept their coin and said, "You made the decision to keep your coin. I have decided you can keep your coin AND get a toy. You don't need to pay for it."

You can imagine this seemed like an amazing deal to the child. He got his gift for free. (I love it when God does this, because I couldn't have planned that someone would opt to keep their money.) It didn't cost him a single cent. He got the toy and the money. The other children were not quite as enthused about this turn of events. But what a perfect example for them of grace. Grace is free. We cannot earn the gift of salvation which comes through God's gift of grace. No, we just receive it. John 1:12 tells us that "Yet to all who did receive him, to those who believed in his name, he gave the right to become children of God..." Just like the child who kept his coin, you get to receive God's blessings. He is going to pour out His grace and His love upon you in abundance. "...to him who is able to do immeasurably more than all we ask or imagine, according to his power that is at work within us... (Ephesians 3:20)" He isn't going to withdraw His love if you don't measure up. He's not keeping score waiting to punish you if you err. No, instead He is saying, Here, I love you so much I'm going to give you all of these blessings AND I'm going to give you an even better gift than you thought possible. I'm going to give you my Son. And it isn't going to cost you a thing. It cost Jesus His life. It cost God His Son's life. It cost us nothing. "For the wages of sin is death, but the gift of God is eternal life in Christ Jesus our Lord. (Romans 6:23)" All we have to do is believe and receive. Please, don't measure God's grace by human standards. He came to earth in the form of a human, but Jesus was all man and all God. His grace far exceeds anything our mind can wrap itself around. And it is for us. It is for you. God's inviting you today. Will you accept the gift He is offering? Will you embrace it? Will you receive this gift for free? No charge? Not only will it change your eternity, but it will change your present. Because once you walk with Jesus, you'll experience a life of grace and love unlimited, joy and peace beyond measure, and an incredible day-to-day journey of being "Kissed by the King."

THE SUN/SON
IS BLINDING

H
ave you ever sat down in a chair only to discover that the sun was coming through the window right into your eyes? It just happened to me. Even when I shut my eyes, I could only see light. In fact, I could even feel the light. Strange, isn't it? We don't just see light, we feel it. I was reminded at that moment that this is the way I want my entire life to be. As a daughter of the King of Kings, I want to see only Jesus. I want to feel the joy that comes in knowing I'm loved unconditionally by the Father. I want to rest in the peace which fills my heart and mind knowing that Christ's blood covers my sin. And to walk daily in the victory under the guidance and filling of God's Holy Spirit.

I looked around trying to figure out how I happened to sit right in that spot. You know what I mean, don't you? If we scooch just a bit to the right or the left, we can see the sun but not be blinded by it. But I question whether that is how we are supposed to live our lives. Are we supposed to see the Son but not allow His love to blind us? Do we want to enjoy the warmth without His vision for life? It is my heart's desire for myself, and you, to walk into any situation in life so full of the Son that we only see Him in it. If the situation is painful, let us see Him. If it is a time to rejoice, we want to see Him.

If we sense evil or danger, we want to view it through the eyes of the authority we have in Christ.

We are learning about the human body this week in preschool. As we looked at the picture in the book yesterday, there was a picture of the shape of the heart and then one of the actual heart that is in a person's body. They are not the same. We were discussing this when one of the children piped up, "Except don't forget our hearts have a door on them!" He felt the author of the book had inadvertently forgotten to include the door. You know the door. It's the door which we open to let Christ in. ("Here I am! I stand at the door and knock. If anyone hears my voice and opens the door, I will come in... [Revelation 3:20]") There was not a doubt in the mind of the children that there should have been a door pictured. And another student expanded on the conversation by reminding everyone we can let Him out again, too. Yep, as we love others, we are sharing Jesus' love with them. The children understand. They carry that childlike faith which views life through the eyes of Jesus. They are blinded by the Son. Will we follow their example? Will we allow ourselves to sit in the direct Sonlight where we view the world around us from His perspective? Are we willing to sit with our eyes closed and be filled with the warmth of His presence? Sure, we can choose a seat where the Son isn't in your eyes, but I question whether we will really be able to see better. Me? I'm going to hang with the little people. They have the right perspective. They view life through the eyes of Jesus!

ABOUT THE AUTHOR

Leslie is a native of Iowa who is in love with Jesus! She loves to share her passion for Christ with children and adults. It was through her love for family, the outdoors, and the joy of a good laugh that the Lord encouraged her to start writing. As He began to reveal Himself through life circumstances and daily events, she realized true joy is found in seeing Him work and hearing Him speak throughout each day. There is no greater joy than to walk side by side with Jesus and allow His Spirit to lead the way. *Kissed by the King* demonstrates that worship is a lifestyle and takes place every time we say, "I see you, Father. Thank you!"

Made in United States
Orlando, FL
24 January 2022

13948632R00147